Current Legal Issues in Publishing

The Acquisitions Librarian Series:

Automated Acquisitions: Issues for the Present and Future, Number 1
The Acquisitions Budget, Number 2
Legal and Ethical Issues in Acquisitions, Number 3
Operational Costs in Acquisitions, Number 4
Vendors and Library Acquisitions, Number 5
Evaluating Acquisitions and Collections Management, Number 6
Collection Assessment: A Look at the RLG Conspectus©, Number 7
Popular Culture and Acquisitions, Number 8
Multicultural Acquisitions, Numbers 9/10
A.V. in Public and School Libraries: Selection and Policy Issues, Number 11
Management and Organization of the Acquisitions Department, Number 12
New Automation Technology for Acquisitions and Collection Development, Numbers 13/14
Current Legal Issues in Publishing, Number 15

Current Legal Issues in Publishing

A. Bruce Strauch
Editor

The Haworth Press, Inc.
New York • London

Current Legal Issues in Publishing has also been published as *The Acquisitions Librarian*, Number 15 1996.

The Haworth Press, Inc., 10 Alice Street, Binghamton, NY 13904-1580 USA

Library of Congress Cataloging-in-Publication Data

Current legal issues in publishing/ A. Bruce Strauch, editor.
p. cm.
"Has also been published as The Acquisitions librarian, no. 15, 1996"–T.p. verso.
Includes bibliographical references.
ISBN 1-56024-804-1 (alk. paper)
1. Authors and publishers–United States. 2. Copyright–United States. 3. Freedom of the press–United States. I. Strauch, A. Bruce. II Acquisitions librarian.

KF3084.C86 1996
346.7304'82–dc20 96-18168
[347.306482] CIP

INDEXING & ABSTRACTING

Contributions to this publication are selectively indexed or abstracted in print, electronic, online, or CD-ROM version(s) of the reference tools and information services listed below. This list is current as of the copyright date of this publication. See the end of this section for additional notes.

- ***CNPIEC Reference Guide: Chinese National Directory of Foreign Periodicals***, P.O. Box 88, Beijing, People's Republic of China
- ***Combined Health Information Database (CHID),*** National Institutes of Health, 3 Information Way, Bethesda, MD 20892-3580
- ***Current Awareness Bulletin***, Association for Information Management, Information House, 20-24 Old Street, London, EC1V 9AP, England
- ***Educational Administration Abstracts (EAA)***, Sage Publications, Inc., 2455 Teller Road, Newbury Park, CA 91320
- ***Index to Periodical Articles Related to Law***, University of Texas, 727 East 26th Street, Austin, TX 78705
- ***Information Reports & Bibliographies***, Science Associates International, Inc., 6 Hastings Road, Marlboro, NJ 07746-1313
- ***Information Science Abstracts***, Plenum Publishing Company, 233 Spring Street, New York, NY 10013-1578
- ***Informed Librarian The,*** Infosources Publishing, 140 Norma Road, Teaneck, NJ 07666
- ***INSPEC Information Services,*** Institution of Electrical Engineers, Michael Faraday House, Six Hills Way, Stevenage, Herts SG1 2AY, England
- ***INTERNET ACCESS (& additional networks) Bulletin Board for Libraries ("BUBL"), coverage of information resources on INTERNET, JANET, and other networks.***
  - JANET X.29: UK.AC.BATH.BUBL or 00006012101300
  - TELNET: BUBL.BATH.AC.UK or 138.38.32.45 login 'bubl'
  - Gopher: BUBL.BATH.AC.UK (138.32.32.45). Port 7070
  - World Wide Web: http: / / www.bubl.bath.ac.uk./BUBL/ home.html
  - NISSWAIS: telnetniss.ac.uk (for the NISS gateway)

  The Andersonian Library, Curran Building, 101 St. James Road, Glasgow G4 ONS, Scotland

(continued)

- ***Library & Information Science Abstracts (LISA),*** Bowker-Saur Limited, Maypole House, Maypole Road, East Grinstead, West Sussex RH19 1HH, England
- ***Library Literature,*** The H.W. Wilson Company, 950 University Avenue, Bronx, NY 10452
- ***National Clearinghouse on Child Abuse & Neglect,*** 3998 Fair Ridge Drive, Suite 350, Fairfax, VA 22033-2907
- ***Newsletter of Library and Information Services***, China Sci-Tech Book Review, Library of Academia Sinica, 8 Kexueyuan Nanlu, Zhongguancun, Beijing 100080, People's Republic of China
- ***NIAAA Alcohol and Alcohol Problems Science Database (ETOH)***, National Institute on Alcohol Abuse and Alcoholism, 1400 Eye Street NW, Suite 600, Washington, DC 20005

SPECIAL BIBLIOGRAPHIC NOTES

related to special journal issues (separates)
and indexing/abstracting

- ❑ indexing/abstracting services in this list will also cover material in any "separate" that is co-published simultaneously with Haworth's special thematic journal issue or DocuSerial. Indexing/abstracting usually covers material at the article/chapter level.
- ❑ monographic co-editions are intended for either non-subscribers or libraries which intend to purchase a second copy for their circulating collections.
- ❑ monographic co-editions are reported to all jobbers/wholesalers/approval plans. The source journal is listed as the "series" to assist the prevention of duplicate purchasing in the same manner utilized for books-in-series.
- ❑ to facilitate user/access services all indexing/abstracting services are encouraged to utilize the co-indexing entry note indicated at the bottom of the first page of each article/chapter/contribution.
- ❑ this is intended to assist a library user of any reference tool (whether print, electronic, online, or CD-ROM) to locate the monographic version if the library has purchased this version but not a subscription to the source journal.
- ❑ individual articles/chapters in any Haworth publication are also available through the Haworth Document Delivery Services (HDDS).

Current Legal Issues in Publishing

CONTENTS

ABOUT THE EDITOR

A. Bruce Strauch is Associate Professor of Business Law at The Citadel where he has been employed since 1977. He practiced tort law for fifteen years and has published numerous articles and books including works of fiction. He is the publisher of *Against the Grain*, a trade journal of the scholarly publishing industry.

ALL HAWORTH BOOKS AND JOURNALS
ARE PRINTED ON CERTIFIED
ACID-FREE PAPER

Introduction

A. Bruce Strauch

The law is too much with us. And for those in intellectual pursuits like publishing, academe, and librarianship, the law is increasingly a part of the daily landscape. This collection of articles has been produced by legal, business, and publishing experts from several different venues. Organized into four broad areas–*Ownership, Fair Use, Licensing*, and *Old Problems Remain*–this collection will shed light on important issues as we wade into the confusing world of copyright, licensing and taxation in the twenty-first century.

OWNERSHIP

Who owns information? The question cannot be answered easily. When it is exacerbated by the fact that information is no longer static (print on paper), but is fluid and transportable (electronic access, downloading, manipulation), the answer becomes even more complex. Is the owner of information the producer of the information (the author), the packager of the information (the publisher or third-party provider, either commercial or non-profit) or some combination of the two? And what right of ownership does a purchaser of the information have?

Ownership is typically defined in terms of copyright law which is designed to encourage creative work by granting authors a monopoly in their product. Literary piracy in the 19th century forced a series of multilateral agreements among nations that resulted in the laws of international copyright we have today (Paul Gleason).

Despite the clear public policy of granting the author ownership, there is always an argument that information should be free or at least govern-

[Haworth co-indexing entry note]: "Introduction." Strauch, A. Bruce. Co-published simultaneously in *The Acquisitions Librarian* (The Haworth Press, Inc.) No. 15, 1996, pp. 1-3; and: *Current Legal Issues in Publishing* (ed: A. Bruce Strauch) The Haworth Press, Inc., 1996, pp. 1-3. Single or multiple copies of this article are available from The Haworth Document Delivery Service [1-800-342-9678, 9:00 a.m. - 5:00 p.m. (EST)].

ment subsidized. With most information publishing being done in the U.S. and Europe, the underdeveloped world is starved for the information it needs (Philip Altbach). Is a society of "haves" and "have nots," as a society, composed of publishers who must be prepared to subsidize the cost so that the "have nots" will be appeased? Should the owners of information be an underfunded society of libraries which wishes to take back copyright from publishers and barter it among colleges and universities (Al Henderson)?

The famous Supreme Court case of *Feist v. Rural Telephone* defined ownership in terms of originality. In the area of database compilations, originality becomes quite fuzzy and conflict cannot be avoided among publishers of similar or identical data (A. Bruce Strauch).

The breadth of ownership encompasses rights to tax deductions. The right to depreciate a subscription list may be key to the bottom line and thus profitability or even survival of a journal or newspaper publisher (Sheila Foster).

FAIR USE

The purchaser of published material must have some right to use it in a practical way or else he has purchased nothing. What rights the purchaser has to use it, reproduce it and distribute it are defined by the doctrine of Fair Use. In this area, the well-known case of *American Geophysical Union v. Texaco* has become a key precedent on the question of archival copying. It is limited however to the for-profit business world and leaves unanswered the question of fair use on university campuses (Todd Parkhurst).

The digital age has not become the death knell of print works. Rather print and electronic materials exist together and are used together. While fair use has typically protected educational activity, multimedia works and a desire by universities to substitute electronic for print have created a confusing landscape (Laura Gasaway).

Does a speaker have an ownership right to his words that can preclude others from reproducing them? What right does a news reporter have to publish those words (Anne Jennings)?

LICENSING

In a world of multimedia deals, authors may no longer treat the licensing of electronic rights as an afterthought. The issues addressed by the

National Writers Union's "Statement of Principles on Contracts Between Writers and Electronic Book Publishers" provide a useful guide for the author (Glen Secor).

The development of a new publishing medium during the life of an existing contract will cause disputes as to what is covered by the license. The now historical conflict between movie and television rights provides an informative background for examining the brewing conflicts over "implied licenses" in the on-line digital world (Charisse Castagnoli).

Can a license cover everything? The ease with which electronic media can be manipulated provides an enormous problem in preserving the integrity of an author's work. Through what are called "Moral Rights," the European Union has developed an area of continuous ownership for the author which does not travel with the copyright or any licensing of it. The U.S. accession to the Berne Convention has brought this by the back door into U.S. copyright law (John Cox).

An owner may retain copyright, yet license specific use rights to other parties. Licensing schemes are seen by many as a solution to the problem of easy widespread distribution that electronic media permits. The electronic media itself will likely permit a solution to the problem it has created. Middlemen that provide indexes and delivery options will soon be in the business of collecting fees for the copyright owners (Rebecca Lenzini/Ward Shaw).

OLD PROBLEMS REMAIN

Even as we push the envelope into an electronic wonderland, the old tort problems of publishing–defamation and obscenity–remain very much with us (Glen Secor).

OWNERSHIP

Major International Copyright Conventions: Their Origins and Main Implications

Paul Gleason

INTRODUCTION

A nation's copyright law serves as a bridge between the world of ideas and the world of commerce.[1] It generally has several purposes: (1) to guarantee an author, a monopoly, or exclusive, right to control the uses

---

Paul Gleason, Assistant Editor with the International Monetary Fund (Washington, D.C.), served as Editor of the *Society for Scholarly Publishing Letter* during 1990-91. He has contributed articles on copyright and international publishing to *Scholarly Publishing, Against the Grain,* and the International Association of Scholarly Publishers' *IASP Newsletter.*

The views expressed in this article are those of the author and should not be interpreted as reflecting the views of his employer, the International Monetary Fund. Portions of this article were previously published, in somewhat different form, in Philip G. Altbach and Edith S. Hoshino, eds., *International Book Publishing: An Encyclopedia* (New York: Garland Publishing, 1995).

[Haworth co-indexing entry note]: "Major International Copyright Conventions: Their Origins and Main Implications." Gleason, Paul. Co-published simultaneously in *The Acquisitions Librarian* (The Haworth Press, Inc.) No. 15, 1996, pp. 5-16; and: *Current Legal Issues in Publishing* (ed: A. Bruce Strauch) The Haworth Press, Inc., 1996, pp. 5-16. Single or multiple copies of this article are available from The Haworth Document Delivery Service [1-800-342-9678, 9:00 a.m. - 5:00 p.m. (EST)].

made of his or her own original work for a specified period; (2) to guarantee an acquiring publisher a monopoly right to print and sell a work for a specified period; (3) to provide financial compensation, or royalties, to authors to reward them for their creative work; and (4) to encourage progress in a country's arts, humanities, and natural sciences in order to encourage its economic, social, and cultural development.

National copyright laws have often created, and continue to create, controversy and sometimes rancorous disputes among authors, publishers, governments, and the larger societies in which all of the foregoing live and work. The granting of a legal monopoly to publishers acquiring copyright in books–which has helped to give them enough confidence in their ability to recover, through sales, their investments in editing, publishing, marketing, and distributing works to justify their running the risks involved in almost any publishing venture–has conflicted with the reading public's "need to know" and its desire for the freest possible flow of information, with publishers' prices for books the principal focus of debate. Such tensions are well-nigh inevitable because although books are physical commodities sold at a particular price, the information they contain is a resource whose value to society is not diminished by the widest possible dissemination.

The term "international copyright" is used to describe the collection of bilateral and multilateral agreements among countries to protect literary and artistic works–a subdivision of intellectual property (works that require intellectual effort to create) that includes books, films, musical compositions, computer software, and many other kinds of works–outside their own borders by harmonizing their respective national copyright laws.

Not long after Gutenberg began experimenting with the use of movable type on a hand-operated printing press, in what is now Germany, in about 1436, both secular and religious leaders, who recognized the potential impact of printed works on public opinion, began to regulate the printing trade. On this point, Ithiel de Sola Pool has observed that "the printing press was a bottleneck where copies could be examined and controlled. In the passage from the author's pen to the reader's hand, the press was the logical place to apply controls, be it to censor sacrilege or sedition or to protect the author's intellectual property."[2] This regulation gradually became more formalized in various European countries, as monarchies were eclipsed by parliamentary systems, and national copyright laws emerged, beginning with England's Statute of Anne in 1710.

Before the nineteenth century, copyright was principally a domestic concern of European countries, with most books circulating primarily within the country where they were both written and published. Book piracy–the production and sale of editions of books that have not been authorized by their authors (copies infringing on the author's rights) in competition with authorized editions–was principally a domestic concern. After 1800, however, profound political changes–such as the rise of the bourgeoisie, the spread of literacy and education, and greater freedom of expression–greatly increased the demand for both literary and artistic works. Publishing expanded rapidly, as did both bookselling and the establishment of libraries. As trade, travel, and communications between countries increased, increasing numbers of books were sold abroad and the problem of international book piracy grew quite serious.

Piracy was widespread not only because of the quick profits it promised but also because intellectual property was still a relatively new concept. During the seventeenth and eighteenth centuries, the idea that it deserved legal protection both domestically and internationally had gradually gained adherents, primarily in Europe. Attitudes in other countries, however, were rather different. For example, in the United States, which adopted its first copyright law in 1790, reprinting European (primarily English) works without either requesting permission or making payment was widespread in the 1800s. Though this was clearly piracy in the eyes of many Europeans, it was completely legal under U.S. law, which then protected only the works of U.S. authors.

DEVELOPMENT OF INTERNATIONAL COPYRIGHT CONVENTIONS

When book pirates operated in a publisher's own country, the publisher could use its domestic copyright law to shut down the pirates' businesses and subject them to penalties, but when pirates operated from another country, the publisher had no recourse unless the two countries happened to have a bilateral copyright agreement. In the first half of the nineteenth century, European countries made extensive efforts to establish a network of bilateral agreements among themselves, based on reciprocity of copyright protection, but the result proved unsatisfactory. Beginning in the 1850s, the idea of a common framework for copyright protection emerged as the favored solution to the problem of copyright enforcement internationally. After extended preliminaries, a series of intergovernmental negotiating sessions held in Berne, Switzerland resulted in agreement being reached on the International Convention for the Protection of Literary and Artistic Works (1886), more commonly known as the Berne Convention.

The Berne Convention was designed to operate on the principle of *national treatment*: essentially, each member country (that is, a country adhering to the Convention) agrees to provide copyrighted works originating in any other member country the same protection that works of domestic origin receive under its own copyright law. It also provides that member countries of the Berne Union (those that adhere to the Convention) must provide a minimum standard of protection–in regard to the content, scope, and duration of copyright–to works originating in all other members.

The Berne Union, which started out with only 14 members, most of which were European, has expanded over the years to 112 members today. The Convention has undergone quite a few revisions, the most important of which took place in Berlin in 1908, Rome in 1928, Brussels in 1948, Stockholm in 1967, and Paris in 1971. Among other changes, the Berlin revision adopted the principle that no formalities (notice, deposit, and registration) would be required in member countries to obtain copyright protection; the Rome revision added the moral rights of authors to the copyright protection already provided for under the Convention; and the Brussels revision increased the minimum permissible period of copyright protection of a work to the lifetime of its author plus 50 years, which remains in effect today.

During the first several decades the Berne Convention was in effect, only two countries from North and South America joined it–Brazil in 1922 and Canada in 1928. A series of inter-American copyright conventions were established during this period, however, including the Montevideo Convention of 1889, the Mexico City Convention of 1902, the Rio de Janeiro Convention of 1906, the Buenos Aires Convention of 1910, the Havana Convention of 1928, and the Washington Convention of 1946. These agreements established the principle of national treatment among their members, but, because they included only countries of the Americas and did not all have the same memberships, the result was widely considered to be unsatisfactory protection of copyrighted works originating in member countries.

The end of World War II, which brought about important changes in international publishing, also ushered in significant changes in international copyright relations. The United States, which had avoided joining the Berne Convention principally because it feared that doing so would involve antagonizing domestic interest groups, emerged as a major publishing power with an increased interest in exporting books. (Although the United States did not join Berne until 1989, U.S. publishers had long been able to have their works protected under the Convention, without accepting the obligations of membership, through the "back door to Berne"–that is, by publishing first editions of books simultaneously in the United States and a Berne member, such as Canada or the United Kingdom.) It began looking into the development of a second international convention that would be acceptable to it; the countries of Latin America; and other countries that–principally because relatively few works were produced by their domestic authors, and because they wanted to make works produced elsewhere as widely and cheaply available to their citizens as possible–did not want to accept all of the obligations involved in joining Berne.

In 1952, the United Nations Educational, Scientific, and Cultural Organization (UNESCO) held a conference in Geneva to discuss the development of such a convention. The result was the Universal Copyright Convention (UCC), which came into effect in 1955. The UCC states that it has three principal purposes: (1) to protect the rights of authors (the only stated purpose of Berne); (2) to ensure respect for the rights of the individual; and (3) to encourage the development of literature, arts, and sciences, as well as the dissemination of works of the mind.

Like the Berne Convention, the UCC is based on the principle of national treatment. Unlike Berne, it does not provide for a minimum standard of copyright protection–a feature that tends to favor net importers of intellectual property over net exporters. The Convention specifies a minimum term of copyright protection for books of the life of the author plus 25 years and requires applicants for copyright protection to comply with a single formality–putting a copyright notice on the work. The UCC, which was signed by 40 countries in 1952, currently has 94 members. It has been revised only once, in conjunction with the revision of the Berne Convention, in Paris in 1971.

DEVELOPING COUNTRIES AND INTERNATIONAL COPYRIGHT

As Europe's colonial empires broke up in the 1940s, 50s, and 60s, large numbers of new, often weak nations appeared and set about the business of fostering their own economic development. Although these nations' resource endowments, climates, infrastructures, education levels, and political philosophies varied widely, they agreed that they needed to obtain scientific, technical, and other information–much of which was in the form of copyrighted works–from the industrial countries if they were to realize their hopes for development. As *The ABC of Copyright,* a UNESCO publication, puts it, "Improvement of living conditions everywhere depends to a large extent on the progress of education, science and culture. Such progress is made possible through the dissemination of information and knowledge and its application to national development."[3]

The prices charged by industrial country publishers for books were (and

are) set based on their own costs–for wages, materials, printing, etc.–and the ability to pay of consumers in their domestic and principal foreign markets (generally other industrial countries). Because copyrighted books published in industrial countries were very expensive, book pirates found ready markets for their unauthorized editions of, for example, popular U.S. or European textbooks. Technological improvements in printing and binding, as well as improvements in both surface and air transportation, made it possible for pirates to operate on a larger scale and to increase their profits. Copyright laws in developing countries were sometimes nonexistent, more often loosely drawn when it came to protection of foreign works, and their provisions tended to be loosely enforced.

Industrial countries, most prominently the United States and the United Kingdom, attempted to meet part of the need of developing countries for affordable (low-priced) books through a variety of foreign aid programs that subsidized the production of reprinted or translated works abroad. Private foundations also provided such assistance. These efforts to satisfy the "book hunger" of developing countries reached their peak during the expansive 1960s, when they financed the delivery of millions of books to developing countries, and have diminished markedly since then as government funding has dwindled. Industrial country publishers also have attempted–and, to a lesser extent, continue to attempt–to cope with piracy of their own books and to satisfy developing countries' book hunger by selling them "international student editions" at prices well below those charged for the same works in their home markets. The above-mentioned book programs clearly have done considerable good, yet they also have been criticized for inhibiting the growth of indigenous publishing industries in recipient countries.

Meanwhile, in meetings of various international organizations–UNESCO, the administrator of the UCC; the United International Bureaux for the Production of Intellectual Property (later succeeded by the World Intellectual Property Organization (WIPO), the administrator of the Berne Convention; and the United Nations Conference on Trade and Development (UNCTAD)–developing countries, using both their combined voting strength and their limited leverage as nonaligned countries during an era of superpower competition, and with the support of some sympathetic publishers and government officials in industrial countries, worked to lessen their inequality with the industrial countries by, among other things, reducing industrial countries' control over information production and distribution.

In the early 1960s, a series of copyright meetings in developing countries suggested that the Berne Convention needed to be modified to give them easier access to copyrighted works originating in industrial countries. At the 1967 Stockholm Conference, agreement was reached, after lengthy and contentious negotiations, on a protocol (annex) to the Berne Convention. The Stockholm Protocol allowed several exceptions to the generally high level of protection provided to the copyrighted works of Berne Union members in order to assist developing countries. Among others, it reduced the term of protection of copyrighted works sought by developing countries from the life of the author plus 50 years to the life of the author plus 25 years; reduced restrictions on materials that developing countries needed for education and research; and provided for compulsory licenses–that is, licenses to use copyrighted works originating elsewhere to be provided by developing country governments to their domestic publishers in consultation with, but not necessarily with the permission of, the publishers or authors holding the rights–to translate or reproduce copyrighted works in return for "equitable payment" in the developing country concerned.

The Protocol ultimately failed to satisfy either developing or industrial countries. Most of the latter refused to ratify it, and national and international publishers' associations intensified their efforts to protect the copyrights held by their (primarily industrial country) members. Since the two groups of countries seemed deadlocked on the Protocol, it was effectively shelved and a joint conference for simultaneous revision of both Berne and the UCC was held in Paris in 1971. The Paris conference worked out revisions of both conventions that incorporated a compromise between industrial and developing countries on the latter's use of copyrighted works for non-profit educational and research purposes.

The Paris revisions, which were ratified in 1974, provided that developing country publishers who were members of Berne and/or the UCC could obtain compulsory licenses from their governments (specifically, their national copyright authorities) to reprint or translate works–subject to more extensive restrictions than had been included in the Stockholm Protocol–the rights to which were owned by copyright holders in the industrial countries that were members of one or both of the two major copyright conventions.

COMPULSORY LICENSING IN PRACTICE

Translated works published under a compulsory license must be used only for teaching, scholarship, or research, while reproduced works published under such a license may be used only in connection with systematic instructional activities. Both kinds of works may not be sold for profit, must be produced in the licensee publisher's own country (except in cases where the country lacks the necessary publishing capacity), and usually may not be exported.

Although developing countries strongly supported compulsory licensing at both the Stockholm and Paris conferences, relatively few developing countries' governments have granted compulsory licenses to their publishers since the Paris revisions came into effect. Although most industrial country publishers have come to accept such compulsory licensing in principle, they generally have sought to head off the issuance of compulsory licenses in developing countries by either issuing a low-cost edition of their own in that market or, more commonly, negotiating a voluntary (conventional) licensing agreement with a local publisher. Also, developing countries' campaign for additional concessions from industrial countries–in publishing and other fields–has met growing opposition from conservative industrial country governments, with the result that it has been effectively, though probably not permanently, halted. Still, the ability of any developing country government belonging to either of the major copyright conventions to enact compulsory licensing legislation and then issue such licenses has increased the leverage of all developing countries in negotiating conventional licenses with publishers from industrial countries.

INDUSTRIAL COUNTRY PUBLISHERS' OFFENSIVE AGAINST BOOK PIRACY

Book piracy continued to expand during the 1960s, 70s, and early 80s as improvements in manufacturing and shipping, as well as strong growth in Asia and some other parts of the developing world, expanded the opportunities for it. While accurate figures on the volume of piracy, like those on other illegal activities, are extremely difficult to obtain, it is clear that total annual losses of all copyright proprietors in industrial countries–including producers of films, videocassettes, audio tapes, compact disks, computer hardware and software, books, etc.–were substantial, amounting to a billion dollars or more in the early 1980s, and book piracy accounted for a sizable fraction of this. Industrial country publishers, and especially those in the United Kingdom and the United States, consequently became sufficiently alarmed to push for, and obtain, strong action by their conservative, pro-business governments to combat piracy.

New legal provisions enacted in developing countries in response to industrial countries' antipiracy efforts have not always been energetically or effectively enforced. Still, considerable progress has been made against book piracy in developing countries, which is now widely seen as declining, though far from eradicated. As printing-press piracy has diminished in recent years, the difficult problem of unauthorized photocopying of copyrighted works in developing countries has received greater attention. Also, as publishers gain experience with new technologies of information dissemination, such as electronic publishing, they are devoting more effort to devising methods to license new kinds of works to developing countries. On another front, conventional forms of book piracy in the countries of Eastern and Central Europe, as well as the states of the former Soviet Union, have been a growing concern over the past few years.

Many industrial country publishers recognize that, ultimately, piracy can only be minimized or eliminated by reducing the economic incentives that originally brought the pirates into publishing. As mentioned previously, in recent decades, enlightened industrial country publishers have responded to piracy (illegal photocopying as well as traditional printing-press piracy) and the Paris revisions on compulsory licensing by making greater efforts both to sell their books at affordable prices and to license their books to be reprinted and translated at more reasonable rates than in the past.

Still, serious areas of conflict remain between industrial country publishers and developing countries. Significant numbers of the former are reluctant to sell reprint or translation rights to publishers in developing countries because this is likely to reduce sales of the original publisher's own edition there. While their insistence on protecting their market shares makes good business sense when viewed from their vantage point, it also often severely limits the opportunities of students, teachers, and professors in developing countries to obtain the information they need and hinders the development of local publishing industries. In what appears to be a hangover from the colonial period, these publishers essentially refuse to view developing countries as anything but markets for their own products, apparently in the hope they can avoid making the adjustments that will be required when these countries develop viable publishing industries of their own.

DEVELOPING COUNTRIES RECONSIDER COPYRIGHT

While industrial country governments have pressed developing countries, with some success, to eliminate piracy of copyrighted works, the latter's own economic and social development, and their desire to advance the interests of their own publishing industries have induced them to change their attitudes toward the international copyright system. As occurred in the United States much earlier, when a country reaches the point where its publishers and authors have substantial numbers of copyrights and export business to protect, it tends to view joining and strictly observing the provisions of the major international copyright conventions in a much more favorable light.

On this point, Dina Malhotra, a veteran Indian publisher and founder of Hind Pocket Books (New Delhi), observes that India–for many years a leading copyright outlaw in the opinion of industrial country publishers–"now has to protect the copyrights of its own nationals as well as foreigners' rights. It also has to seek protection internationally for its own copyrights for books and audio- and video-tapes, which have also become victims of widespread piracy in many Asian countries."[4] Quite a few other countries, including China, Korea, Taiwan, and other newly industrializing economies of Asia are currently in the process of shifting their stances on international copyright issues for similar reasons. It can certainly be argued that conversions based on a country's perceived self-interest rather than its desire for self-preservation in the face of industrial country sanctions are more likely to last and to induce it to carry out sustained copyright enforcement efforts.

COPYRIGHT PROTECTION AND THE URUGUAY ROUND AGREEMENT

Industrial country publishers, long disgruntled about what they view as substandard protection of their copyrights under Berne and the UCC, have supplemented their efforts to combat piracy over the past decade and a half with efforts to persuade their countries' generally conservative governments to use their leverage in relevant international organizations to press for better protection. During the eight-year Uruguay Round of multilateral trade negotiations, which took place under the auspices of the General Agreement on Tariffs and Trade (the GATT, which is headquartered in Geneva) and was concluded in April 1994, they worked to include intellectual property under the GATT for the first time. The Final Act of the Uruguay Round came into effect on schedule in January of 1995, at which time the new World Trade Organization (WTO) succeeded the GATT.

Industrial country negotiators were largely successful in efforts to achieve agreement on their three principal goals: (1) standards of protection to be based on the standards included in the Berne Convention, (2) standards of enforcement that would ensure accessible civil remedies and strong criminal penalties for piracy, and (3) a dispute-settlement mechanism allowing countries to bring intellectual property disputes before GATT dispute-settlement panels. During the negotiations, most developing countries opposed the spreading of copyright jurisdiction to encompass not only WIPO and UNESCO but also the GATT, primarily because they feared that the dispute-settlement would be used against them, thereby reducing their already limited access to the copyrighted works of industrial countries.

The Final Act set up a Council for Trade-Related Aspects of Intellectual Property Rights, informally known as the TRIPS Council, to monitor the Uruguay Round agreement's operations and governments' compliance with it. It also includes a most-favored-nation clause requiring any participating country that grants a concession, in an agreement on intellectual property rights, to nationals of another country to immediately grant the same concession to nationals of all other participating countries. Developed (industrial) countries have until the end of 1995 to bring their domestic legislation and practices into conformity with the Final Act's provisions. Developing countries are allowed longer transition periods: developing countries and countries in transition from centrally planned to market-based economies will have 5 years, and the least developed (poorest) countries will have 11 years, from January 1, 1995 to achieve conformity.

It will not be possible, however, to know how international flows of copyrighted materials will actually be affected by implementation of the Final Act's provisions, including the dispute-settlement mechanism, until a good deal of experience with them has been gained.

MEMBERSHIP IN BERNE CONVENTION EXPANDS

Although the 1971 Paris revisions brought the Berne Convention and the UCC closer together, substantial differences between them have remained. Though there has been some support, especially in Europe, for merging the two conventions, this has not happened, primarily because of continuing differences between industrial and developing countries. The unhappiness of the United Kingdom and the United States with UNESCO since the late 1970s, which was reflected in their withdrawal from the organization (though both remain members of the UCC, which UNESCO administers) and which has abated somewhat in recent years; the U.S. decision to join the Berne Convention in 1989; and the Uruguay Round agreement, with its explicit link to the provisions of Berne, have certainly created some doubt about the UCC's continuing relevance as a major international copyright convention.

After the United States joined Berne, several countries in both Latin America and the Caribbean and Africa also did. China, a longtime holdout from the international copyright system, joined both the UCC and Berne in 1992. The Russian Federation, which maintains UCC membership as one of the successor states to the former Soviet Union (which joined that convention only in 1973), is expected to join Berne in the not-too-distant future. Now that all major countries are largely within the international copyright system, and formal negotiations are well under way on a proposed new protocol to the Berne Convention, it has become quite clear that, as Philip Altbach wrote in 1986, "despite the stresses, some piracy, and the lukewarm adherence of some Third World nations, the international copyright system appears to be accepted as the basic structure to regulate the international flow of knowledge."[5]

NOTES

1. Edward W. Ploman and L. Clark Hamilton, *Copyright: Intellectual Property in the Information Age* (London and Boston: Routledge & Kegan Paul, 1980), p. 1.
2. Ithiel de Sola Pool, *Technologies of Freedom* (London and Cambridge, Massachusetts: Belknap Press of Harvard University Press, 1983), pp. 16-17.
3. United Nations Educational, Scientific, and Cultural Organization, *The ABC of Copyright* (Paris: UNESCO, 1981), p. 67.
4. Dina N. Malhotra, "Publishing and Copyright in India," *Rights,* Vol. 5, No. 4 (1991-92), p. 1.
5. Philip G. Altbach, "Knowledge Enigma: The Context of Copyright in the Third World," Chap. 6 in Philip G. Altbach, *The Knowledge Context: Comparative Perspectives on the Distribution of Knowledge* (Albany, New York: State University of New York Press, 1987), p. 112.

BIBLIOGRAPHY

Altbach, Philip G., *The Knowledge Context: Comparative Perspectives on the Distribution of Knowledge* (Albany, New York: State University of New York Press, 1987).

_________, "The Subtle Inequalities of Copyright," Chap. 1 in *Copyright and Development: Inequality in the Information Age,* ed. by Philip G. Altbach, Bellagio Studies in Publishing, No. 4 (Chestnut Hill, Massachusetts: Bellagio Publishing Network, 1995).

Childs, William M., and Donald E. McNeil, eds., *American Books Abroad: Toward a National Policy* (Washington, D.C.: Helen Dwight Reid Educational Foundation, 1986).

Patterson, Lyman Ray, *Copyright in Historical Perspective* (Nashville, Tennessee: Vanderbilt University Press, 1968).

Ploman, Edward W., and L. Clark Hamilton, *Copyright: Intellectual Property in the Information Age* (London and Boston: Routledge & Kegan Paul, 1980).

Publishing Research Quarterly, Special Issue on International Copyright, Vol. 8, No. 2 (Summer 1992).

United Nations Educational, Scientific, and Cultural Organization, *The ABC of Copyright* (Paris: UNESCO, 1981).

The Subtle Inequalities of Copyright

Philip G. Altbach

Copyright is well entrenched in international publishing, and yet it faces significant challenges. On the surface, copyright has never been stronger. The concept is increasingly accepted worldwide, and even those Third World countries, such as India, that argued against the inequalities of the international copyright system in the 1960s have largely ceased their opposition. Even China has joined the international copyright system. While piracy has not ended, it has gone underground in all but a few countries. Massive pressure from the United States and Britain has brought such former pirates as Korea, Taiwan, and Singapore into the fold. Perhaps most important, the concept of copyright is almost universally accepted by governments and by those involved in the book trade worldwide.

Copyright has been strengthened by strong governmental pressure from the major publishing countries and from the legal systems in these countries. Copyright has been seen as much as a means of protecting trade advantages as it has as a basic concept of knowledge distribution. The United States and Britain have been concerned about the loss of 'knowledge products' of all kinds (of which books are now only a minor part) because these losses contribute to ever-growing negative trade balances.

The fact is that the printed word, which is the concern of this essay, has been lost in the campaign to protect profits on computer software, compact

---

Philip G. Altbach is Professor of Higher Education and Director of the Center for International Higher Education at Boston College, Chestnut Hill, Massachusetts. He is also Director of the Research and Information Center of the Bellagio Publishing Network, an effort to assist publishers in Africa and other developing areas. Dr. Altbach is co-editor of *International Book Publishing: An Encyclopedia* and other publications.

[Haworth co-indexing entry note]: "The Subtle Inequalities of Copyright." Altbach, Philip G. Co-published simultaneously in *The Acquisitions Librarian* (The Haworth Press, Inc.) No. 15, 1996, pp. 17-26; and: *Current Legal Issues in Publishing* (ed: A. Bruce Strauch) The Haworth Press, Inc., 1996, pp. 17-26. Single or multiple copies of this article are available from The Haworth Document Delivery Service [1-800-342-9678, 9:00 a.m. - 5:00 p.m. (EST)].

disks, films, and other products is a problem for both publishers and readers, since books and journals present special circumstances that require attention. Further, the courts have been increasingly zealous in their protection of copyright and the prerogatives of the owners of knowledge products. For example, in the United States, the courts have narrowly construed copyright regulations in favor of publishers and against those who have claimed 'fair use' in reproducing materials for academic purposes. These rulings have significantly increased the power of copyright owners.

GATT AND INTELLECTUAL PROPERTY

The recently completed negotiations over GATT (General Agreement on Tariffs and Trade) has further entrenched copyright and has created a new means of litigation and control, the World Trade Organization. Intellectual property is a central part of GATT, and GATT enforcement arrangements now join those of the Berne Convention and the Universal Copyright Convention. The products of the mind are considered as commercial property, to be bought and sold in the marketplace. Few see any difference between knowledge products and any other commodity. GATT enshrines the idea that those who bring knowledge products to the marketplace should be able to completely control them.

It is time to take a step back from rampant commercialism to examine the complex world of copyright and the distribution of knowledge. There is, in reality, a difference between a Mickey Mouse watch, a Hollywood film, or even a computer software program, on the one hand, and a scientific treatise, on the other. Textbooks, technical reports, and research volumes are subject to the same copyright regulations as a novel by James Clavell. Those who control the distribution of knowledge treat all intellectual property equally–and are perfectly happy to deny access to anyone who cannot pay. The legal structures set up to protect intellectual property benefit the owners. There is no consideration of the user. The attitude seems to be: No pay, no play.

But even in the marketplace of intellectual property, there was room for negotiation during the GATT deliberations. The French successfully argued that there should be limitations on the free flow of American cultural products to Europe because of a fear of inundation by Disney and Rambo. The French had influence, and a compromise was reached. There are, thus, some "non-market" restrictions allowed in GATT. But no such compromises were permitted for those countries that depend on knowledge products from the industrialized nations and cannot afford to pay the going rates for them. There are no provisions in place to ensure that developing countries can have access to books and other knowledge products.

As it stands, GATT is a blunt instrument which will inevitably work to the disadvantage of poor nations in terms of access to knowledge. Modifications in the current straitjacket imposed by GATT and by the copyright treaties do not mean a rejection of free trade or the idea of a global market-based economy.

TECHNOLOGICAL CHALLENGES

Yet, all is not secure in this era of narrowly construed copyright. Perhaps the greatest challenge to traditional copyright is technology. Every new technological advance brings a flurry of litigation and efforts by copyright owners to limit access to new technologies until their rights can be fully protected. A recent example of this was the fight over digital audio tape (DAT) technology. The widespread dissemination of DAT was held up for several years while the producers of DAT machines and the owners of copyright (mainly the recording companies) struggled over how to ensure that copyright owners would be protected. Photocopiers have posed a continuing challenge to copyright owners and, while the courts have consistently ruled in favor of the publishers, the battle lines are forever changing as new and more sophisticated reprographic technologies are introduced. Data networks are also a new area of contention for copyright holders. How can knowledge products be controlled in an era of instantaneous communication through computer-based networks?

Currently, the most perplexing issues relate to computer programs, computer-based communications networks such as the Internet, and related technological spin-offs. Owners, in this case software companies, database operators and the like, are concerned that the ownership of such innovative technologies be clear, and that non-sanctioned use be prohibited and punished where it occurs. Trade-related intellectual property (TRIPS) has been among the most debated topics in the GATT negotiations. While books and other traditional knowledge products are hardly at the frontier of technology, they have been swept up in the campaign to strengthen ownership.

RECENT DEBATES

It is significant that these battles are over technological innovations. The debate over copyright principles raged in the 1960s and 1970s over issues relating to the appropriateness of control over knowledge and what responsibilities the rich countries had to help build up the educational and scientific systems of the newly developing nations of the Third World. Few argued for the abolition of copyright but many felt that knowledge should be shared more freely and that the industrialized nations, in part because of their earlier colonial domination of the Third World, had special responsibility to assist in the process of development. Some charged the industrialized countries with purposely maintaining tight control over knowledge products in order to keep the Third World in a dependent relationship and to maximize profits. In the ideologically charged Cold War era, charges of neocolonialism were leveled against the major Western countries, and many argued that Western policies were aimed at continuing domination rather than assistance. UNESCO, through its advocacy of a 'new world information order', weighed in on the side of the Third World critics, enraging Western governments and contributing to the withdrawal of the United States and Britain from the organization.

It was said, for example, that Western publishers preferred to export relatively small numbers of books to the Third World rather than grant reprint rights because more profits could be obtained from direct exports. Some claimed that the foreign aid programs of such countries as France, Britain and the United States were aimed at exporting books and ideas rather than at encouraging indigenous development in Third World countries.

The vociferousness of the debates has abated, but the issues remain important. Most realized that the issues were not mainly ideological in nature and are highly complex. India, one of the main critics of the traditional copyright system, found itself emerging as a major producer of books and, not wanting to harm its future export markets, shifted its posture on copyright issues. Most realized that anarchy in the knowledge business would serve no one's long-term interests and that a workable copyright system is necessary and international cooperation a good idea. With the slow winding down of the cold war, most realized the slogans could not change reality. Countries that stood outside the copyright system, including the Soviet Union and China, slowly joined it.

PATTERNS OF INEQUALITY

Yet, it is important to realize that the international knowledge system is highly unequal, and it can be argued that those who are in control of the system–and specifically copyright arrangements–have a special responsibility to assist in the intellectual and educational development of the Third World. There is a kind of OPEC of knowledge in which a few rich nations and a small number of multinational publishers have a great deal of control over how and where books are published, the prices of printed materials, and the nature of international exchange of knowledge. These same forces tend to dominate the new information and knowledge dissemination technologies. Because the knowledge infrastructures are located in these countries, there is a kind of monopoly that has been difficult to break. And because knowledge is not a finite natural resource but is infinitely expandable, there is the possibility of more countries becoming members of the cartel. There has, in fact, been relatively little expansion in the number of knowledge producing countries–and the price of entry into the cartel increases as the cost and complexity of knowledge production goes up.

Copyright, from its beginnings in England in the sixteenth century, has been a means of protecting the "haves"– of limiting access to books and information in order to maintain order and discipline in the trade–of creating a monopoly over knowledge. There are, of course, very good arguments in favor of copyright. These include the principle that those who create and disseminate knowledge and knowledge products should economically benefit from these creations and that the creator should maintain some basic control over the creation. Also inherent in the idea of copyright is that intellectual creativity should also benefit society–this is indeed the underpinning of copyright as expressed in the American Constitution.

THE RESPONSIBILITY OF COPYRIGHT

Along with power, and copyright bestows considerable power on the copyright holder, comes responsibility. For the most part, those who hold most of the world's copyrights and who also control the international copyright system have been largely concerned with power–with maintaining control over their copyrights and with maximizing their economic benefits. Copyright is seen in purely legal and economic terms. There is virtually no recognition that there are inherent non-economic factors involved in copyright and that those who hold power now have a responsibility to assist those who do not have access to the world's knowledge. Copyright, after all, is a moral and ideological concept as well as a legal and economic one. There is no recognition that the legacy of colonialism and the power of the multinationals has, to a significant extent, created the current highly unequal world knowledge system. It is, of course, much easier for the "haves" to cling to the economic and legal underpinnings of a system that has given them a virtual monopoly over the world's knowledge products than to recognize that we live in an interdependent world and that the Third World desperately needs access to knowledge and technology. In the current context, it is unlikely that those who need access to knowledge most will be able to obtain it "at current market rates" any time soon. What is needed now is affirmative action to ensure that books and other knowledge products are not kept from Third World nations because of the restrictions of the copyright system. Copyright holders must now spend time thinking about the needs of Third World readers in addition to their concerns about maintaining market share. In the broader scheme of things, providing the assistance that is needed to the Third World will not cost very much. Indeed, in terms of copyright, the main requirement is largely access to permissions, rights, and a very small amount of market share.

A necessary first step is increased consciousness of the complex issues relating to the world's knowledge system and the role of copyright in it and a recognition that a broader perspective is needed. A modest amount of economic sacrifice may also be required along with some inconvenience. Copyright must not be seen in isolation from issues of access to knowledge, the needs of Third World nations, and the broad history of colonialism and exploitation. It is not productive to point fingers or assess blame for past inequities. Rather, we must quickly move toward copyright arrangements that will maintain the copyright system while at the same time permit flexibility so that the needs of the "have nots" can be met. The needs are indeed great, and they are not limited to the poor countries of the developing world. For example, Moscow's famed Lenin Library is no longer purchasing any scientific journals from the West because there is no allocation of 'hard currency' funds. Few, if any, other libraries or academic institutions in the former Soviet Union are able to obtain access to key books and journals in the current circumstances. The situation is even more desperate for many sub-Saharan African countries, where purchases of books and journals from abroad ceased several years ago because of lack of funds. Some countries lack the facilities to produce many kinds of books and must rely on supplies from abroad. These countries, and the number is depressingly long, are probably in more desperate need now than a decade ago. The end of conflicts in such countries as Cambodia, Laos, Uganda, Angola, Ethiopia, and others has permitted them to turn their attention to the rebuilding of educational and library systems, and there is a desperate need for books of all kinds as well as for the equipment and expertise to build up indigenous publishing capacity. Economic crisis throughout Africa has created special needs exacerbated in some ways by the emergence of fledgling democratic regimes in some countries that must improve the lives of their citizens if they are to survive. Books are a small but highly visible way of making such improvements. Further, access to knowledge may help to build up a commitment to democratic ideals. Countries in the former Soviet Bloc, from Mongolia and Vietnam, to the Czech Republic and Bulgaria, need speedy access to the world's knowledge, having been cut off from much of it for almost a half-century.

The specific needs vary greatly. In some cases, access to scientific journals and books at subsidized prices for a limited period would help greatly. In others, local publishers with limited markets need easy and inexpensive access to foreign books in order to translate them into the local language. In a different context, permission to reprint books from the industrialized countries in the original language is needed to serve an indigenous population literate in English or French but unable to pay the high cost of imported books. And for some countries, most of the elements of an indigenous publishing industry are missing and there is a need to build it up from scratch. Copyright may not be the key element in all of these circumstances, but it does play a role.

Responsible world citizenship with regard to copyright is unlikely to be extraordinarily costly. Countries and publishers that require special assistance on copyright issues are unlikely to be major customers in any case—markets tend to be small and purchasing power very limited. Yet, there will be some costs involved. Export sales may be modestly reduced and income from the sale of rights foregone or limited. There may also be some administrative costs for industrialized country publishers. But the long-term benefits might well outweigh the immediate costs and inconvenience. A self-sufficient book industry in a Third World country is likely to be a better partner, and in the long term a better customer as well, than would a weak and demoralized publishing community. Further, as the Indian case has shown, self-sufficient publishers tend to be supporters of copyright because they see adherence to copyright in their best interest.

It may be worth recalling that copyright compliance comes naturally with economic and social development. One of the most egregious violators of copyright in the nineteenth century was the United States, which felt, probably incorrectly, that it could build up its domestic publishing industry most effectively by freely reprinting works from abroad while protecting the rights of domestic authors. Once American publishing was well-developed, the United States became a defender of copyright. Until the 1960s, the Soviet Union had a similar perspective. International copyright was violated as the country used knowledge from abroad for its own purposes. China has had a similar perspective up to the 1990s and has only recently joined the international copyright system. Nations must see copyright as in their best national interests before they become fully supportive of it.

WHAT CAN BE DONE?

There are a number of steps that can be taken to help developing countries gain access to the world's knowledge and also build up their own indigenous publishing industries. None require a violation of the basic principles of copyright and, in the long run, will strengthen it because more countries will see it in their best interest to support copyright.

There must be a recognition that all knowledge products are not the same, and that while it may be justified to insist on commercial terms for Nintendo games, some flexibility for scientific materials, textbooks and the like is appropriate. The owners of knowledge must modify their purely profit-oriented approach to certain segments of the knowledge industry.

Permissiveness in copyright relations in the short run may yield more profits in the long run for owners. For example, a publisher may obtain less money by licensing a book for a local edition in Africa or a translation in Asia than by exporting copies. In the long run, however, a viable domestic publishing industry and a literate public will buy ever-increasing numbers of books.

The idea of compulsory licensing–providing to Third World countries the automatic right under some very limited circumstances to reprint or translate Western books with the payment of reduced fees–was pressed by Third World representatives at international copyright meetings in the 1960s, and after considerable debate and cajoling, and significant watering down by the "copyright powers" was finally ratified by most Berne Convention and UCC members, and came into effect in 1974. The concept is a sound one so long as it is kept within carefully limited guidelines. Compulsory licensing permits Third World publishers quick access to relevant educational and scientific materials by permitting them to reprint or translate materials for educational and a few other uses. The Third World publisher would be required to inform the copyright holder and provide some payment, often at below-market rates. In fact, compulsory licensing is not widely used. This arrangement removes much of the bureaucracy from the system and also permits Third World readers to have access to knowledge from abroad fairly quickly. One of the common complaints from Third World publishers is that many Western publishers simply do not respond to requests for reprint or translation rights. Charging fees that are clearly beyond the ability of Third World publishers to pay is another common problem.

In the past decade, the copyright "powers" have used every means available to ensure strict compliance with both the spirit and the letter of international copyright treaties and with national copyright laws. One of the most successful tactics used to ensure copyright compliance has been to link it to broader trade arrangements. American copyright holders, for example, have pressured their government to threaten countries who do not enforce copyright with the withdrawal of trade preferences. These threats had a role in convincing such major U.S. trading partners as Taiwan and Singapore to cease most pirating. China is currently facing severe trade sanctions by the United States because of its refusal to cease pirating computer software, CDs, and related products. GATT has further linked copyright to the world trade system. While these efforts have yielded some results in terms of immediate compliance, it can be argued that copyright must be "sold" on its own merits, that it is as much a moral issue as a commercial one, and that making copyright hostage to international trade, an arena where Third World nations have little leverage in any case, is in the long run detrimental to the emergence of a copyright system based on consensus and mutual understanding.

Western publishers must take a long-term view of world publishing. This means their policies must permit offering inexpensive access to books and journals for reprinting and translation. There is a feeling in the Third World that Western publishers often simply ignore the requests of Third World publishers and institutions because there is little money to be made and discussions often become complex and sometimes acrimonious. Western publishers must respond positively and quickly to requests and understand the problems faced by Third World publishers.

Joint ventures or cooperative arrangements with indigenous publishers in the Third World may help both sides. The Western publisher provides expertise, products, and sometimes capital. In return, access to markets is opened up. Such ventures must be on the basis of equality, and autonomy for Third World partners is important. There are many kinds of joint ventures, ranging from a major involvement to cooperation on specific projects. Many involve work together on issues relating to copyright.

The book trade relationships between the industrialized nations and the Third World are unequal. Books are exported from the West to the Third World. Copyright permissions are requested by Third World publishers and are sometimes granted by counterparts in the West. There is very little traffic in the other direction. It may be possible to significantly increase the import of books from developing countries and thus strengthen Third World publishers significantly. It may also be possible for Western publishers to obtain rights to Third World books for publication and distribution in the West. Because most of the world's books are published in the major industrialized countries, the unequal relationship will continue, but there may be ways of ameliorating it to a modest extent. It is important to keep in mind that what is a modest transaction to a Western publisher may be a significant development to a Third World firm.

CONCLUSION

Copyright is, in a way, symbolic of the relations between the 'haves' and 'have nots' in publishing. All of the cards are in the hands of the Western publishers. They control the international copyright treaties, which were, after all, established by them and with their interests in mind. The Western publishers dominate the world book trade. The powerful multinational publishers, which are Western-controlled, reach into many countries. In the post-Cold War era, Western governments have increasingly threatened trade sanctions as a means of protecting a narrow interpretation of intellectual property. GATT and its enforcement agency, the World Trade Organization, provide powerful new weapons in this struggle. While the major beneficiaries have been software producers, film companies and the like, book publishers have also benefited, and have strongly supported these initiatives. Copyright is widely respected internationally and, at least for books, is more tightly enforced than has been the case in the past.

The time has come to recognize that the production of books and journals is more than a business, and that trade in knowledge and knowledge products is somehow different than commerce in automobiles or coconuts. Those who control knowledge distribution have a responsibility to ensure that knowledge is available throughout the world at a price that can be afforded by the Third World. I am not advocating overthrowing the copyright system, or even weakening it. I am arguing for a broader understanding of the responsibilities of publishers in a complex and unequal world. Such an understanding will, no doubt, require some rethinking of the relationships between the knowledge 'haves' and 'have nots.' In an era of interdependence, this is not an altogether bad thing. It is likely to be controversial and perhaps unpopular. No one with power likes to share it. But if the immense challenges of Third World development are to be solved, publishers and other owners of intellectual property will have to play a modest role.

University Ownership of Faculty Copyrights

Albert Henderson

The "Information Age" is now at its half-century mark. As it develops and evolves at a seemingly ever faster rate, a new assault on the legal underpinnings of information has been launched by the managers of one segment of the huge R&D knowledge industry. Various groups of librarians and university managers, ranging from the relatively informal Triangle Research Libraries Network (TRLN) to the well-established Association of Research Librarians (ARL) and American Association of Universities (AAU), have supported the proposal, which they prefer to describe as a model policy covering faculty publication in scholarly journals. If adopted, it would involve universities in the business of copyright to an extent not imagined 20 years ago when the current copyright law was implemented.

The present proposals are presented as the solution to a crisis. In the letter covering their 1992 draft, the TRLN group explains that they seek a remedy for the horrendous level of subscription cancellations forced upon impoverished academic libraries. The *Reports* of the AAU Research Libraries Project (RLP) (1994) echo this concern in far greater detail and cite numerous studies of journal prices and library economics, many of which also describe a state of crisis. The common thread of these propositions is to call for university ownership of copyrights in the research articles

---

Albert Henderson, Editor of *Publishing Research Quarterly,* provides business consulting and training services to publishers and other organizations. He is not an attorney and makes no attempt to give legal advice. Address for correspondence: Box 2423 Noble Station, Bridgeport CT 06608-0423, INTERNET: 70244.1532@compuserve.com.

[Haworth co-indexing entry note]: "University Ownership of Faculty Copyrights." Henderson, Albert. Co-published simultaneously in *The Acquisitions Librarian* (The Haworth Press, Inc.) No. 15, 1996, pp. 27-33; and: *Current Legal Issues in Publishing* (ed: A. Bruce Strauch) The Haworth Press, Inc., 1996, pp. 27-33. Single or multiple copies of this article are available from The Haworth Document Delivery Service [1-800-342-9678, 9:00 a.m. - 5:00 p.m. (EST)].

written by their faculty. The advantage to universities would be that their libraries presumably would not have to pay royalty fees for copies of articles controlled by the consortium (ibid:141-143). Nor, presumably, would they subscribe to the journals that publish the articles in question.

While the TRLN presentation consists of a letter signed by 8 members of a committee representing the three universities Raleigh-Durham-Chapel Hill area, the AAU/RLP document runs 153 pages. It includes over 60 bibliographic references, a number of figures, and exhibits the names of over 40 task force members. Lest there be any confusion whether this is about money, the chart titled "monographs and serials costs in ARL libraries 1986-1993" is presented twice. Undoubtedly the issues are more complex than they appeared to be two years earlier. In fact, they are more complex than the latest presentation would have us believe.

A great deal of information has been omitted from these presentations, not the least of which is some projection of cost requirements and the likelihood of achieving measurable goals including income and savings that would justify the investment. The starting point of feasibility would be to answer the question: To what degree will ownership of copyrights in faculty articles address the projected costs of increased royalty fees resulting from subscription cancellations? My own analysis suggests that the proposal, which focuses largely on the science and technology literature, will never control a sufficient share of copyrights to pay for itself. The U.S. accounts for a little more than one third of world authorship according to National Science Board figures. The U.S. generates only about 22 percent of the world literature in chemistry, about 30 percent of physics papers, and larger shares in other major fields. Because U.S. authors cite U.S. authors twice as often as they cite foreign authors, chances are they also order copies in a higher proportion. Therefore, we might reasonably project that one-half of all articles of interest might potentially come under the purview of the AAU/RLP proposal. There are exclusions, of course. First, exclude the great number of science papers originated by government and industry employees. Exclude to some degree the increasing number of papers authored jointly. National Science Board figures indicate that 11 percent of the world's articles were co-authored internationally, about double the percentage of a decade earlier. The bottom line here is that the proposal can potentially control no more than 10 to 20 percent of all papers of interest. The copyrights in the majority of papers authored outside the United States would be beyond the reach of the AAU/RLP. Furthermore, as Zahray and Sirbu (1989/90) have pointed out, there is every reason to believe that publishers will raise fees on the remaining copyrights sufficiently to offset all of the savings envisioned by university managers. Zahray and Sirbu even predicted the development of the AAU/RLP proposal as the outcome of the classic "prisoner's dilemma," whereby the cooperation of all is organized to solve a common problem and fails.

The AAU/RLP report skips around several major landmarks on the copyright horizon: the 1976 Copyright Act, the CONTU protocol (calling for libraries to subscribe to any journal they ordered 5 or more articles from), and the court decisions against the "fair use" claims of Kinko's, Texaco, and Michigan Document Services, all of whom attempted to make photocopies without paying royalties. Academic photocopying classified as interlibrary "loans" increased by a factor of 5 or more during the 1980s. By 1987, when the Register of Copyrights took testimony on photocopying under the new law, it was no secret that photocopying, justified tenuously as "fair use," had been substituted for thousands of canceled library subscriptions to the consternation of both association and commercial publishers. Is publishers' legal complaint of copyright infringement inevitable? The language of the law (Section 108(g)) suggests the basis for such a suit:

> Provided, That nothing in this clause prevents a library or archives from participating in interlibrary arrangements that do not have, as their purpose or effect, that the library or archives receiving such copies or phonorecords for distribution does so in such aggregate quantities as to substitute for a subscription to or purchase of such work.

In this light, the AAU/RLP proposal might be seen as a legally sophisticated attempt to develop a consensus to be used eventually to argue in their defense should a complaint be filed in Federal court. Their position expresses the new claim that the universities produced the research and so they actually should own it legally; it is unfair that they must purchase it again. In other words, faculty writings have always belonged to the universities. Now they feel the universities should have control because they now have the means to do so. Here is a rather 'balkan' gambit which, as in the game of chess, seeks to control the center of the board at the expense of considerable otherwise unproductive administrative effort. The argument fails because it is made possible only by recent technology; if it had merit today it would have had merit ever since the 17th century when the first copyright laws were passed and the basis for such intellectual property began to develop.

Among the peculiarly interesting suggestions made by the AAU/RLP task force is the clarity of the proposal (15ff.) to acquire, digitize and maintain within a "delivery system" at least one copy of every foreign publication of academic interest. The proposal suggests that library collection development funds be diverted to resource sharing in order to support this venture. Once acquired, digitized and cataloged, these works will be copied for distribution to the entire academic community. The AAU/RLP task force neglects to contemplate the likelihood that such works are protected, presumably, under the Berne Convention. The reach of the law is considerable and the mood of enforcement should be recognized. In the midst of drafting this article, I received an announcement from Association of American Publishers (AAP) indicating their victory over the pirating of copyrighted works in China, the outcome of a legal action taken by AAP in Beijing. The AAU/RLP must come to grips with the likelihood that foreign publishers and authors will protect their rights in the enormous United States market, particularly when the aggregate harm would quickly reach mammoth levels and the intent can be easily proved through documentary evidence. I also wonder whether this proposal to monopolize distribution of foreign works by the same organizations that operate dozens of university presses might well lead to complaints alleging restraint of trade. This is an area in which university presses compete with commercial and other nonprofit publishers. My long experience in the import/export market tells me that its implementation certainly would have an impact on many U.S. publishers' interest in acquiring North American rights to and importing foreign works.

The downgrading of the academic library market has already had a devastating impact on publishers' allocation of resources. One of the unexplored economic consequences of the proposals would be further chilling of publishers' investments in research-level products. Review journals, monographs, handbooks, encyclopedias, bibliographies, abstracts, indexes, databases, and other "secondary" publications are designed to guide the researcher and student through the overwhelming mass of research activity. Unlike articles that report the results and methodology of primary research, secondary publications are initiated largely by publishers who invite, encourage, and recruit editors and authors. The writing and editing is rarely supported by research grants. Many are undertaken entirely as entrepreneurial responses to perceived market needs. These are highly specialized information products for which academic libraries have always provided the major (in some cases the only) market. The AAU/RLP proposal (p. 19) mistakenly suggests that faculty and researchers will embrace their plan when they understand the ease of identifying, locating and getting a copy of any item. The Achille's Heel of the plan is that it actually will eliminate the market for reviews and guides that digest the literature and support the researcher's first requirement: "identifying items of interest." The work product of primary research, filed like dissertations and never indexed or reviewed, will rarely get the inspection and analysis that relieves each researcher of the need to duplicate the process in order to identify items of real interest. Moreover, without convenient, well-organized library collections, researchers cannot rely on the method of systematic browsing, held by many faculty as preferable to the use of bibliographic tools (Dougherty, 1991).

In sum, here is the fundamental issue that the AAU/RLP task force panels have failed to address: the greatest challenge to researchers over the last 100 years or more has been to keep up with and understand progress in all fields of interest. Over the last 50 years numerous committees and commissions have raised with some urgency, but not solved, this issue and the related problem of sharing and standardizing primary data, whether it be physical, social, or health data. While calculators have generally eliminated the need for most mathematical tables common a generation ago, researchers still look to the initiative of publishers to prepare and publish data that will eliminate the costly duplication of laboratory and field work.

Without a robust library market, publishers are inclined to place their resources elsewhere. Machlup and Leeson (1978) noted that the average print run of academic publications had started decreasing, an economic factor that every university press director will report has continued to this day. As a matter of survival, established presses have narrowed their editorial coverage to focus on mainstream research. Many have sought out new foreign, regional, business, and trade markets. Publishers of the most successful science journals have seen their library circulation fall by half (Henderson, 1994/95, 1995). Publishers of abstracts and indexes have also narrowed their coverage, responding to library cancellations (Kaser, 1995). Demands by academic librarians for electronic versions of print formats have further taken their toll on research publishers. By allocating scarce resources to investigate and experiment with digital media, publishers have further reduced the time and money available for editors, authors, marketing, and promotion. Meanwhile, the gurus who follow Viacom, Time-Warner, Sony, etc., all have indicated that a revolution is coming in the ways that digital communications and computers are used to deliver information. The huge consumer interest in home shopping, sports, and sitcoms-on-demand services will probably result in far-reaching changes. The technological notions expressed in the AAU/RLP proposal and elsewhere within the research community will soon be not only obsolete but probably premature as investments by academic libraries and publishers.

In terms of bottom line analysis, the real crisis is not the cost of the journal subscriptions or even of all library costs. It is the productivity and effectiveness of the services rendered by the university. If universities are to survive, the impact of decimated library collections on the effectiveness of education and research can no longer be ignored. It must be squarely faced. Poor library performance will not be solved by a technological solution that deliberately avoids the fundamental needs of researchers, organizational causes of distress, and centuries of development of property rights. The library crisis cannot be separated from the financial history of the universities that control 70% of library materials purchasing power in the United States. *Digest of Education* (1993, Tables 332 and 335) figures for public and private universities 1977-1991 provide the following picture:

Administration to libraries	+ 32%
Administration to instruction	+ 13%
Research to instruction	+ 10%
Administration to research	+ 2%
Libraries to instruction	– 14%
Libraries to research	– 22%

The tilt of these ratios is no mistake. It is simply unexplained. In 1991 constant dollars, universities are spending over $500 million more on their administration than they did a generation ago. With the bureaucracy appearing to cannibalize financial support for libraries and instruction, an explanation is overdue. As a red herring to draw attention away from this basic cause of libraries' deteriorating performance, the present proposal is not unrelated to the infamous public relations canard–staging a conflict between instruction and research–which achieved coverage by Leslie Stahl on the 60 Minutes television show not long ago. In this light, the true conflict we see would be the contest for money between the bureaucracy and the universities' mission-oriented components. Therefore, the AAU/RLP task force appears to be no more than a dog-and-pony show to sell another justification of expanded administrative payrolls. There is no real benefit to the researcher, the student, or the teacher. Nowhere in the TRLN, AAU/RLP or related documents is it explained how photocopies of uncertain legal status can serve the library patron better than a good, up-to-date collection.

NOTES

Association of American Universities. Research Libraries Project. 1994. Reports of the AAU Task Forces on acquisition and distribution of foreign language and area studies materials; A national strategy for managing scientific and technological information; Intellectual property rights in an electronic environment. Washington DC: Association of Research Libraries. 1-27, 28-98, 101-153, respectively.

Dougherty, Richard M. 1991. Needed: user-responsive research libraries, in *Library Journal.* 116,1 (Jan.):60-62.

Henderson, Albert. 1994-95. The bottleneck in research communications, in *Publishing Research Quarterly.* 10,4 (Winter):5-21.

Henderson, Albert. 1995. Research journals: a question of economic value, in *Logos.* 6,1:43-46.

Kaser, Richard T. 1995. Secondary information services. Mirrors of scholarly communication, in *Publishing Research Quarterly.* 11,3 (Fall): 10-24.

Machlup, Fritz, Kenneth W. Leeson and associates. 1978. *Information through the Printed Word: The Dissemination of Scholarly, Scientific, and Intellectual Knowledge.* New York: NYU Press. 4 vols. 1. Book Publishing. 2. Journals. 3. Libraries. 4. Books, Journals and Bibliographic Services.

National Science Board. 1993. *Science & Engineering Indicators 1993.* Washington DC: National Science Foundation.

Zahray, W. Paul, and Marvin Sirbu. 1989/90. The provision of scholarly journals by libraries via electronic analysis: an economic analysis, in *Information Economics and Policy.* 4:127-154.

After *Feist*: How Small Is Minimal? The Idea/Expression Merger

A. Bruce Strauch

The 1991 U.S. Supreme Court Case of *Feist Publications Inc. v. Rural Telephone Service Co.*[1] caused a great stir in the publishing world by eliminating the "sweat of the brow" doctrine from copyright law and substituting minimal creativity. It was interpreted, perhaps rightly, as laying open to copying all manner of expensively-produced compilations of data. Companies or individuals who had spent time and money compiling directories for sale in the marketplace felt they could suddenly be faced with competing products that leeched off their efforts. Mere "sweat of the brow" was no longer enough to give a company copyright over a product.

In fact, *Feist* had a limited impact in that sweat of the brow was never a universal rule. The split of authority that was resolved by the *Feist* case grew out of the fact that the Copyright Act of 1909 made no reference to originality. Rather, §3 granted copyright protection to the "copyrightable component parts" of the author's work but neglected to identify originality as the key to distinguishing what was protected from what was not.

Additionally, "composite and cyclop'dic works, directories, gazetteers, and other compilations" were specifically named as being copyrightable.[2] This led to an argument that compilations were protected *per se* which was intellectually justified by the "sweat of the brow" or "industrious collection" theory. In 1922, a line of "sweat" cases began with a disputed directory of jeweler's trademarks in *Jeweler's Circular Publishing Co. v. Keystone Publishing Co.*,[3] and produced the much quoted:

[Haworth co-indexing entry note]: "After *Feist*: How Small Is Minimal? The Idea/Expression Merger." Strauch, A. Bruce. Co-published simultaneously in *The Acquisitions Librarian* (The Haworth Press, Inc.) No. 15, 1996, pp. 35-45; and: *Current Legal Issues in Publishing* (ed: A. Bruce Strauch) The Haworth Press, Inc., 1996, pp. 35-45. Single or multiple copies of this article are available from The Haworth Document Delivery Service [1-800-342-9678, 9:00 a.m. - 5:00 p.m. (EST)].

> The man who goes through the streets of a town and puts down the names of each of the inhabitants, with their occupations and their street number, acquires material *of which he is the author.*[4]

Authority divided between whether copyright protection turned on the labor involved in compiling the data,[5] or upon the originality of the arrangement of the data,[6] and even resulted in the 1977 case of *Schroeder v. William Morrow & Co.*,[7] in which both legal theories were cited as though identical. *Feist* resolved this in favor of originality.

The criticism of the "sweat of the brow" theory is that it afforded copyright protection to the facts themselves. Thus, a publisher confronted with facts already compiled, either had to pay for their use or start from scratch.[8] Yet it was precisely "such wasted effort that the proscription against the copyright of ideas and facts . . . [is] designed to prevent."[9] Facts and ideas were not to be locked up, but were to be made available for all to use.

The 1976 Copyright Act clarified this in Section 103(b) saying that copyright protection for compilations "extends only to the material contributed by the author of such work, as distinguished from the preexisting material employed in the work, and does not imply any exclusive right in the preexisting material."

Interestingly, Section 103(a) defines compilations as works:

> formed by the collection and assembling of preexisting materials or of data that are selected, coordinated, or arranged in such a way that the resulting work as a whole constitutes an original work of authorship.[10]

Feist supposedly put the matter to rest. The case involved a white pages telephone directory with alphabetized names, residences and phone numbers. Feist Publications, Inc., in creating a broad, area-wide directory, copied from a narrow, local directory. In keeping with the language of the 1976 Copyright Act, the Supreme Court held that originality sparked copyright protection and not the effort involved in compilation.

The public policy behind copyright law, however, is "to stimulate [the creation of useful works] for the general public good" by granting the author a fair return for creative labor.[11] The Court was confronted with the problem that no one would break a sweat to create easily stolen products, and thus useful compilations of data would never get made. It tried to resolve this by requiring only a minimal amount of originality, saying:

> [o]riginal, as the term is used in copyright, means only that the work was independently created by the author (as opposed to copied from other works), and that it possesses at least some minimal degree of creativity. To be sure, the requisite level of creativity is extremely low; even a slight amount will suffice. The vast majority of works make the grade quite easily, as they possess some creative spark, 'no matter how crude, humble or obvious' it might be.[12]

A commonly seen result of *Feist* is phone books with business listings in a separate section from residential. This is a total nuisance to the phone book user but ostensibly protects the publisher's product. The originality is severely minimal. [13]

IDEA/EXPRESSION MERGER: MULTIPLE MODES OF EXPRESSIONS

The fundamental principles of copyright are sound. If facts belonged to the discoverer or the compiler, they could be locked up and denied to the public. If ideas could be owned, there would be no free-flow of ideas. It is the expression and not the fact or the idea which is afforded copyright protection.[14]

But what if there is only one way of expressing an idea? The Court found in *Feist* that the alphabetical listing of names and phone numbers was "not only unoriginal but practically inevitable." The minimal level of creativity was not achieved. The level of creativity was indeed non-existent. How does a publisher know when a compilation has fallen to that unoriginal level of arrangement?

The "merger doctrine" purports to deal with the noncreative compilation by merging idea and expression with idea coming out the winner–i.e., no copyright protection. Expression merges with idea when "there are no or few other ways of expressing a particular idea."[15] This prevents anyone acquiring a monopoly on the underlying "idea" or "art."[16] On the other hand, "if the same idea can be expressed in a plurality of totally different manners, a plurality of copyrights may result."[17]

The preferred view is that originality determines copyrightability and the merger doctrine is used to determine if infringement has occurred.[18] While this may seem like arcane legal reasoning, it at least gives an orderly approach to the problem.

Matthew Bender & Co. v. Kluwer Law Book Publishers[19] was a 1987 case in the U.S. District Court for the Southern District of New York. This was a pre-*Feist* case, but in a jurisdiction where originality and not sweat of the brow was the controlling factor for copyright protection.

Matthew Bender published a nine volume set *Damages in Tort Actions* in which one volume contained in chart form personal injury/wrongful death awards in similar cases. This would be used as a guide by lawyers to estimate the worth of a particular suit. Subsequently, Kluwer published a one volume work *Guide to Current Personal Injury Awards and Settlements*. There were numerous similarities between the two volumes, although the cases reported–the fact situations giving rise to damages–were mostly different.

The Court did not deal with a question of originality which is now key after *Feist*, but certainly the culling and selecting of cases to report meets the originality requirement. Rather the issue as considered was whether Matthew Bender could have a copyright in a particular chart with chapter and sub-chapter headings as an expression of an idea. To determine this, it had to apply the merger doctrine.[20]

The Court found that while the "expression" of tort action damages could be done in various ways, there were limited categories for grouping the information. Basically, the information to be grouped was parties, lawyers, location of trial, fact situation and award or settlement. Prior to Bender's work, American Law Reports ("ALR"), American Jurisprudence ("AmJur") and Corpus Juris Secundum ("CJS") had grouped personal injury cases in the same fashion.[21] Since Bender's categories are simply common sense, idea and expression merged, and Bender could not hold a copyright on them.

Educational Testing Services v. Katzman[22] is a much cited case in which merger was denied. ETS is the developer and administrator of the Scholastic Aptitude Test (SAT) as well as Achievement Tests in many subject areas. ETS registers its tests for copyright protection under a "secure test" registration which only requires that the test be identified without a complete copy of the test being provided. Katzman ran a test prepping service which acquired under mysterious circumstances advance copies of tests about to be administered.

Citing test question cases, the Court found the ETS test questions to be original works of authorship.[23] Katzman argued for merger of idea and expression, claiming a limitation on the number of ways the idea can be expressed. The Court, however, citing its own holding in *Apple Computer* held "[i]f other methods of expressing that idea are not foreclosed as a practical matter, then there is no merger."[24]

The Court was very skeptical of the notion that there was a limit to the number of ways students could be tested on "square roots or dangling participles." So no merger, and ETS has copyright protection.

IDEA/EXPRESSION MERGER: THE ABSTRACTIONS TEST

The famous Judge Learned Hand is credited with having formulated the "abstractions test" in *Nichols v. Universal Pictures Corp.*[25] The case grew out of a copyright dispute between a play "Abie's Irish Rose" and a movie "The Cohens and the Kellys." Both had the theme of marriage between Irish Catholic and Jew, family squabbles and ultimate reconciliation that followed. Other than that, the stories were very different.

Judge Hand noted that a plagiarist lifting a block of material–a literal appropriation–was a much easier matter for determination than one who took an abstract of the whole. Two plots may have many general patterns of similarity, "but there is a point in this series of abstractions where they are no longer protected, since otherwise the playwright could prevent the use of his 'ideas,' to which, apart from their expression, his property is never extended."[26]

It no doubt adds nobility to a legal doctrine to cite Judge Hand as the origin, but his holding–the more remote the abstraction from an original, the less likely it is an infringement– is not a true test. Indeed, in Hand's last copyright case, *Peter Pan Fabrics, Inc. v. Martin Weiner Corp.*, he asserted there was no principle for when idea moves into expression and all decisions were of necessity ad hoc.[27]

In its current form, the "abstractions test" merges idea and expression depending upon the level of abstraction at which the idea is formulated. At a low level of abstraction–I prefer apples to oranges or sheep to goats–idea and expression will not merge and thus will be protected. However, a high level of abstraction–Einstein's Theory of Relativity–will merge idea and expression, and Einstein will hold no copyright. [28]

The denial of protection to "building block ideas"–i.e., high abstractions–is supported by Section 102(b) of the Copyright Act which denies protection to any "idea, procedure, process, system, method of operation, concept, principle, or discovery." A Copyright Office Circular 31 spells out a denial of copyright protection for:

> . . . ideas or procedures for doing, making, or building things; scientific or technical methods or discoveries; business operations or procedures; mathematical principles; formulas, algorithms; or any concept, process [or] method of operation.

While this is a more difficult concept to grasp than the single versus multiple modes of expression test, the two do nonetheless correspond. In each, ideas are being kept in the public domain while an author can possess his particular statement of an idea. Unless . . . there's only one way of stating the idea.

In the area of data compilations, the abstractions test is reasonably practical. Selection of facts or data on the basis of taste and personal opinion are protected—not because the sweat work is more worthy, but because the loss of free use to the public carries little danger. A compilation of the most valuable baseball cards to collect or the "right" families for a social register fall into this category. [29]

Selection of facts as a component part of an analysis to reach a precise result or a better-than-average probability of that result should probably not be protected. A medical list of symptoms that predict a disease are building blocks for prediction. The idea should remain free for the public to use.

AFTER FEIST: MIDDLE GROUND ABSTRACTIONS

Kregos v. Associated Press[30] was actually argued before *Feist*, but by the time the opinion was rendered, it was post-*Feist*, and *Feist* was cited by the Second Circuit as affecting its ruling.

Since the 1970s, George Kregos has syndicated a pitching form to newspapers which lists data on the past performance of pitchers who will play in the day's game. There are nine categories with such information as won/lost record and earned run average. In 1984, the Associated Press began publishing a nearly identical pitching form on its own. As the pitching data itself is uncopyrightable facts, the issue was Kregos' right to the particular categories of data which he selected to present.

The District Court held that given the limited space in a newspaper, the possibilities for selecting and presenting differing pitching statistics were extremely small. Due to the severe limitation, the requisite minimal originality was not met by Kregos and the expression and idea merged. Kregos should not have copyright protection. This is the limited modes of expression test. Only one way to say it—not protected.

Using the "abstractions test" the District Court judge found that Kregos was publishing an "outcome predictive pitching form."[31] The pitching data was building blocks—a component part of an analysis to reach a precise result. At that high level of abstraction, it effectively lost copyright protection through merger of idea and expression. With this analysis, Kregos also lost.

The Appellate Court recognized that originality was the first threshold and found that originality in Kregos having nine pitching performance statistics while all prior forms had only three. This also got them past the limited mode of expression test because nine versus three shows that past performances of pitchers can be measured by a variety of statistics. [32]

When the Appeals Court applied the "abstractions test," it likewise arrived at a different result. It analyzed the issue as falling in the middle of a spectrum between pure taste and an analytical formula for prediction.

"He (Kregos) is doing more than simply saying that he holds the opinion that his nine performance characteristics are the most pertinent. He implies that his selections have some utility in predicting outcomes."[33]

But as Kregos provided no system for using the data, the Court analogized to horse racing statistics where every race track gambler would apply his own system. Kregos had not crossed the line into the area of determinable probability of outcome. Thus he was within the taste and preferences area and had copyright protection.

AFTER FEIST: AUTOMOBILE RED BOOK

CCC Information Services Inc. v. Maclean Hunter Market Reports, Inc.[34] was provoked by *Feist* and tracks with *Kregos,* as they are both Second Circuit cases. A publisher produces an *Automobile Red Book* which is a compendium of used car valuations sold in three regions of the United States.

For a number of years, a computer data base service loaded the *Red Book* onto its network and "republished" the information. The *Feist* ruling prompted the data service to seek a declaratory judgment as to liability under the copyright laws. Data base service contended that while the *Red Book* contains fairly complex data involving value adjustments for mileage, for various options on the cars, and for make, model number, body style and engine type–it is nonetheless a collection of facts–not ideas.

The District Court read *Feist* as requiring a high level of originality for protection, contrary–as the Appellate Court noted–to the clear language of the case. *Feist* holds that originality is to be found except in "a narrow category of works in which the creative spark is so utterly lacking as to be virtually nonexistent."[35]

Given the correct reading of *Feist*, the *Red Book* publisher prevailed on the originality issue. The threshold was met by the publisher making valuation predictions for the used car market by region. The valuations were not preexisting facts like in *Feist.* Rather, these predictions were professional judgments based upon economic and sales conditions in the respective areas.

Other aspects of originality were the selection of optional features, adjustment for mileage in 5,000 increments, and the creation of an abstract concept of the "average" car for each category as a point of comparison. The Court further noted the low level *Feist* type requirement of originality it had established in *Key Publications, Inc. v. Chinatown Today Publishing Enterprises, Inc.*,[36] where a narrow selection from a broad list of businesses of interest to Chinese-Americans was given copyright protection.[37]

What is particularly of interest about *CCC Information* is the way it dealt with the "idea-expression" dichotomy. The data base service argued that the *Red Book* was an expression of the author's ideas–his idea of the value of each car. There is only one way to express such an idea, e.g., two thousand dollars (or $2,000, if you will). Therefore the idea merges with the expression and is not protected by copyright law. If any one of these "ideas" could be taken, then data base service did nothing wrong in taking all of them.

The Court rejected this reasoning, finding that it would deny protection to compilations which had been specifically granted by Section 103 of the Copyright Act. Using the *Kregos* low-level of abstraction analysis, the *Red Book* valuations would fall within the category of opinion and would therefore be protected. The valuations were not building blocks of understanding. They "explain nothing, and describe no method, process, or procedure."[38] There would be no injury to the public by requiring that their use be licensed and paid for.

UNCERTAINTY IN COMPILATIONS REMAINS

Copyright law aims for a balance between competing interests–broad dissemination of materials versus fair material rewards for the creative artist.[39] The Supreme Court's approach in *Feist* was to focus on the arrangement of material in the compilation. Given some minimal creativity in arrangement, the public would have access to facts with a wholesale copying being prevented. Nonetheless, the creativity requirement will continue to be a problem in the area of large compilations. The arrangement of accumulated data is by function.

> [S]ince the narration of history must proceed chronologically–or at least, such is the convention–the order in which the facts are reported must be the same in the case of a second supposed author. There cannot be any such thing as copyright in the order of presentation of the facts . . .[40]

Trying to apply the outcome in *Kregos* to the *Matthew Bender* case is particularly mind-boggling. Limited mode of expression? Yes, the Court found that the categories of parties, lawyers, location of trial, fact situation and award/settlement to be just common sense, i.e., the only one way to do it. So no copyright protection.

Applying the building blocks test, you hit the middle level of the spectrum just like *Kregos*. The publisher is saying his litigation data has some utility in predicting outcomes, but the data is not part of a real system for predicting outcomes. So the publisher gets copyright protection.

This is a great game for lawyers working for billable hours, but a very uncertain marketplace for publishers of compilations. All the torturous reasoning of idea-expression merger will not pull us away from the fact that it is the industrious compilation that deserves the reward and not some trivial novelty in arrangement. Even the theory that originality lies in selecting and culling the data breaks down when confronted with the exhaustive compilation. With the touch of a computer key, an exhaustive list of lawyers in the United States could be changed from state-by-state to legal specialties or types of practice or region. Original expression by arrangement shifts to another original expression by arrangement.

Fair Use analysis focuses on economic harm to the copyright holder by a user of the data. Commercially exploiting a data base–reproducing it without adding a socially valuable creative element–is an infringement.[41]

If authorship were found in the very act of pulling data together in a mass, then the whole analysis would be vastly simplified. The only question then would be whether a use of it was fair use and the measure of monetary damages, if any.[42]

NOTES

1. 499 U.S. 340, 59 LW 4251 (1991).
2. ch. 320, § 5(a) Stat. 1076 (1909).
3. 281 Fed 83 (2d Cir.), cert. denied, 259 U.S. 581, 42 S.Ct. 464, 66 L.Ed. 1074 (1922).
4. *Id.* 281 Fed. at 88. (Italics supplied.)
5. e.g., *Leon v. Pacific Telephone & Telegraph Co.*, 91 F.2d 484, 486 (9th Cir. 1937).
6. e.g., *Triangle Publications, Inc. v. Sports Eye, Inc.*, 415 F.Supp. 682 (E.D.Pa.1976); *Simms v. Stanton*, 75 Fed. 6,13 (C.C.N.D.Cal.1896).
7. 566 F.2d 3.
8. *Miller v. Universal City Studios, Inc.*, 650 F.2d, at 1372.
9. *Rosemont Enterprises, Inc. v. Random House, Inc.*, 366 F.2d 303, 310 (CA2 1966), cert. denied, 385 U.S. 1009 (1967).

10. 17 U.S.C. § 103(a).

11. *Twentieth Century Music Corp. v. Aiken*, 422 U.S. 151,156 (1975); *See* England's Statute of Anne of 1710, "An Act for the Encouragement of Learning, by Vesting the Copies of Printed Books in the Authors or Purchasers of Such Copies" for the origin of Anglo-American copyright.

12. 499 U.S. at 345 (citations omitted).

13. *See Northwestern Bell Telephone Co. v. Bedco of Minnesota, Inc.*, 501 F. Supp. 299, 301-302 (D.Minn.1980); *see also Grolier, Inc. v. Educational Reading Aids Corp.*, 417 F.Supp. 665, 667-68 (S.D.N.Y.1976) (original compilation of children's reading materials).

14. *See Mazer v. Stein*, 347 U.S. 201, 217, 74 S.Ct. 460, 470, 98 L.Ed. 630 (1954); *Baker v. Selden*, 101 U.S. 99, 105 (1897); 17 U.S.C. §102(b) (1982); *see also Reysher v. Children's Television Workshop*, 533 F.2d 87, 90 (2d Cir.1976).

15. *Apple Computer, Inc. v. Franklin Computer Corp.*, 714 F.2d 1240, 1253 (32d Cir.1983), *cert. dismissed*, 464 U.S. 1033,104 S.Ct. 690, 79 L.Ed.2d 158 (1984).

16. See M.B. Nimmer, *Nimmer on Copyright* § 2.18[c] at 2-202 to -204 (1985).

17. 714 F.2d at 1253 (quoting *Dymow v. Bolton*, 11 F.2d at 690, 691 (2d Cir.1926)).

18. 3 *Nimmer on Copyright* § 13.03[B][3] at 13-58 (1990).

19. 672 F.Supp. 107 (S.D.N.Y. 1987).

20. *Id.* at 109.

21. *Id.* at 110-111.

22. 793 F.2d 533 (3rd Cir. 1986).

23. *Id.* at 539; See *Association of American Medical Colleges v. Mikaelian*, 571 F.Supp. 144, 150 (E.D.Pa.1983) (medical school admission test), *aff'd*, 734 F.2d 3 (3d Cir.1984); *National Conference of Bar Examiners v. Multistate Legal Studies, Inc.*, 495 F.Supp. 34, 36 (N.D.Ill.1980) (bar examination), *aff'd in part, rev'd in part*, 692 F.2d 478 (7th Cir.1982), *cert. denied*, 464 U.S. 814, 104 S.Ct. 69, 78 L.Ed.2d 83 (1983).

24. *Id.* citing *Apple supra at* 1253.

25. 45 F.2d 119,121 (2d Cir.1930), *cert. denied*, 282 U.S. 902, 51 5.Ct. 216, 75 L.Ed. 795 (1931).

26. *Id.* at 121 citing *Holmes v. Hurst*, 174 U.S. 82, 86,19 S.Ct. 606, 43 L.Ed. 904; *Guthrie v. Curlett*, 36 F.(2d) 694 (C.C.A.2).

27. 274 F.2d 487,489 (2d Cir.1960). *See also Lotus Dev. Corp. v. Paperback Software Int'l*, 740 F.Supp. 37, 60 (D.Mass.1990).

28. *See* William F. Patry, *Copyright Law and Practice*, 312-325 (1994); Melville B. Nimmer & David Nimmer, *Nimmer on Copyright*, §13.03[A][B] (1994).

29. *See Eckes v. Suffolk Collectables v. C.P.U.*, 575 F.Supp. 459 (E.D.N.Y. 1983) *rev'd sub. nom., Eckes v. Card Prices Update*, 736 F.2d 859 (2d Cir.1986); see also *Social Register Ass'n v. Murphy*, 128 F. 116 (C.C.D.R.I.1904); *see also New York Times Co. v. Roxbury Data Interface, Inc.*, 434 F.Supp. 217, 222 n. 2 (D.N.J.1977).

30. 937 F.2d 700 (2nd Cir. 1991).

31. *Id.* at 706 citing 731 F.Supp. 113,119 (S.D.N.Y.1990).
32. *Id.*
33. *Id.* at 707.
34. 44 F.3d 61, 63 USLW 2375, (2nd Cir. 1994).
35. 499 U.S. at 359.
36. 945 F.2d 509, 514 (2d Cir.1991).
37. 44 F.3d at 66.
38. *Id.* at 73.
39. *United States v. Bily*, 406 F. Supp. 726, 730 (E.D. Pa. 1975).
40. *Myers v. Mail & Express Co.*, 36 Copy. Dec. 478 (S.D.N.Y. 1919) (Hand, J.).
41. *See The Parody Defense to Copyright Infringement: Productive Fair Use After Betamax*, 97 Harvard L. Rev. 1395,1399 (1984).
42. *See* Denicola, *Copyright in Collections of Facts: A Theory for the Protection of Nonfiction Literary Works*, 81 Colum. L. Rev. 516, 525 (1981).

Depreciation of Customer-Based Intangibles: *Newark Morning Ledger* and Beyond

Sheila D. Foster

INTRODUCTION

One of the basic principles of proper accounting is the matching of revenues with the expenses that produced those revenues. This principle governs the accrual of revenues and expenses, the use of accounts payable and accounts receivable, and the booking of prepaid expenses and deferred liabilities and credits. Depreciation and amortization[1] have been specifically addressed in the U.S. Tax Code (*Code*) as methods of matching revenues and expenses. Under Section 167 (*§167*), the taxpayer is allowed a deduction for the wear and tear, obsolescence, or exhaustion of assets used in a trade or business or held for the production of income. Although the *Code* specifically addresses only tangible assets, the accompanying Treasury Regulations (*Regs*) state that an intangible used in a trade or business or held for the production of income may also be depreciated if the intangible has a limited useful life that can be estimated with reasonable accuracy.

Sheila D. Foster is Assistant Professor in the Department of Business Administration at The Citadel in Charleston, SC 29409. Ms. Foster is a licensed Certified Public Accountant. She is a graduate of Radford University and has earned an MEd in Guidance and Counseling from Virginia Commonwealth University and a PhD in Accounting from Virginia Polytechnic Institute and State University. Dr. Foster teaches financial and mangerial accounting and writes in the areas of accounting and auditing education, taxation, and ethics. She lives in Charleston with her two sons, Eric and Jason.

[Haworth co-indexing entry note]: "Depreciation of Customer-Based Intangibles: *Newark Morning Ledger* and Beyond." Foster, Sheila D. Co-published simultaneously in *The Acquisitions Librarian* (The Haworth Press, Inc.) No. 15, 1996, pp. 47-59; and: *Current Legal Issues in Publishing* (ed: A. Bruce Strauch) The Haworth Press, Inc., 1996, pp. 47-59. Single or multiple copies of this article are available from The Haworth Document Delivery Service [1-800-342-9678, 9:00 a.m. - 5:00 p.m. (EST)].

It has been said that assets, once used, begin the " 'march to the rubbish heap' ."[2] From this point of view, it seems logical to treat most assets as an expense that occurs over time. Difficulty arises over the depreciation of tangibles when the assets appreciate in value over time and with use. The justification for expensing assets while those assets rise in value is less clear. Rather than representing an expense to be matched with revenues, these assets, it could be argued, are producing income in that the value of the asset is greater at the end of the period than at the beginning.

However, although it is possible to find examples of assets whose values increase over time, most assets decrease in value either with use or over time through wear, obsolescence, or supersession by technologically superior alternatives. Much like prepaid expenses, they are assets that will provide benefit and whose value will decrease over an extended period of time as they are employed in a trade or business.

With tangible assets, the amount of depreciation expense is affected by the estimated useful life of the asset, the length of time that the asset can be used, or the number of units of activity that the asset can produce. For financial statement purposes, useful life is estimated based upon the experience of the user. For tax purposes, useful lives are generally legislated. For example, a company may estimate the useful life of an automobile to be seven years *(length of time)* or 50,000 miles *(units of activity)* and use that estimated useful life for calculating depreciation expense for the income statement issued as part of the annual reports to the SEC and its shareholders. The *Tax Code,* however, under both ACRS *(Accelerated Cost Recovery System)* and MACRS *(Modified Accelerated Cost Recovery System),* has ruled that the useful life of that automobile for tax purposes is three or five years. This results in different depreciation expense being reported for financial and tax purposes. However, in both cases, an attempt is made to match the expense of purchasing an automobile with the revenues generated as the automobile is used in the business.

In a similar manner, most intangibles are governed by laws that establish a limited legal life for each category of assets. Unless the company believes that the useful life is shorter, the legal life becomes the useful life for both financial and tax purposes. A patent, for example, has a legal life of seventeen years. If the owner deems that the patent will be useful for fewer than seventeen years, then that shorter useful life would be used for determining amortization expense. However, even though in some cases the patent might be valuable to the company for more than seventeen years, patent laws make the useful life measurable by placing a limit on the legal life. As required by the *Tax Code,* an end to the useful life of the asset can be seen with reasonable accuracy from the beginning, and the rationale for expensing that asset over its useful life is clear.

Not all intangible assets, however, have been depreciable–at least in the eyes of the Internal Revenue Service *(IRS)*. The *Regs* to Section 167 state that no depreciation is allowed for an intangible whose useful life is not limited. The *Regs* state specifically that goodwill, an asset with an unlimited useful life, may not be depreciated. Therefore, while companies with goodwill on their books as a result of a purchase may depreciate that goodwill over a period of not more than forty years for their financial statements, no deduction for depreciation has been allowed for the goodwill for income tax purposes. This can result in significantly different amounts of income being reported on the financial statements and the income tax return.

The nondepreciable status of goodwill was upheld first in the 1926 case of *Red Wing Malting Co. v. Willcuts* (1927 *CCH* ¶7024 [CA-8, 1926]). The court found that goodwill suffered no wear and tear, did not become obsolete, was not used up in operations, and was, therefore, not subject to depreciation.

With the limited guidance provided by the *Code* and *Regs,* another asset-group that has generated a great deal of discussion and disagreement between taxpayers and the IRS is the cost of acquiring customer-based intangibles such as subscriber lists, customer lists, insurance expirations, and bank core deposits. If these assets are viewed as intangibles with limited lives that can be reasonably estimated, a deduction for depreciation should be allowed; however, if they are viewed as elements of goodwill, no deduction would be allowed. Much litigation has been initiated over these intangibles, and confusion has resulted from conflicting court decisions. The differences often have been based upon the manner in which a particular court has defined goodwill.

When addressing the issue of depreciating customer-based intangibles, the courts have defined goodwill two ways with two different results. When the courts have defined goodwill as expected continued patronage, depreciation of these intangibles has been disallowed. However, when the courts have defined goodwill as the residual value after accounting for assets of ascertainable value and determinable useful lives, depreciation of customer-based intangibles often has been permitted.

CUSTOMER-BASED INTANGIBLES AS GOODWILL

The question then is what constitutes goodwill. The *Code* and the *Regs* do not define goodwill. Therefore, the courts have undertaken to develop a definition. In *Grace Brothers v. Commissioner,* goodwill was defined as "the sum total of those imponderable qualities which attract the custom (*sic.*) to the business–what brings patronage to the business" (49-1 *USTC* ¶9181). In *Boe et al. v. Commissioner,* where the intangible under dispute was approximately 9,000 contracts for medical service, the court decided that these contracts were " . . . terminable at will, and their value depends entirely upon the expectation that they will not be terminated–that is, the expectancy of continued patronage." As such, even though the taxpayer testified that the contracts lasted for variable periods with customers dropping out because they were "unhappy" or "have died," the court ruled that the contracts could not be viewed as a capital asset that diminished in value each time a patient was terminated, and no value could be assigned to each termination. The court expanded the judicial definition of goodwill in stating that, "[to] us, the essence of goodwill is the expectancy of continued patronage, for whatever reason" (62-2 *USTC*, ¶9699).

In *Commissioner of Internal Revenue v. Killian* (63-1 *USTC* ¶9347), the court again addressed what constituted goodwill and stated that "the nature of goodwill . . . is the expectancy that 'the old customers will resort to the old place' " (quoting from the opinion of Lord Eldon in *Cruttwell v. Lye*, 17 *Ves. Jr.* 335, 346, 34 *Eng. Rep.* 129, 134 [Ch 1810]). The courts have held that goodwill " . . . enables the purchaser to step into the shoes of the seller" (*Balthorpe v. Commissioner of Internal Revenue* [66-1 *USTC* ¶9187]), and that "[it] is immaterial that the agreement did not use the term 'goodwill,' for [t]he use of these words is, of course, not necessary if in fact what is transferred does give to the purchaser everything that can effectively aid him to step into the shoes of the seller' "(*Masquelette's Estate v. Commisioner of Internal Revenue* [57-1 *USTC* ¶9267]).

Based upon these and other earlier cases, in *Golden State Towel and Linen Service, Ltd. et al. v. U.S.*, the court used the "mass asset rule" under which customer lists, although arguably distinct assets, were viewed as "inextricably" linked to goodwill. In this case, the court was even more emphatic that customer lists were goodwill and stated that "one [is] a mirror reflection of the other, for goodwill = expectancy of continued patronage = customer lists = goodwill." The court went on to say that "[a] normal turnover of customers represents merely the ebb and flow of a continuing property . . . and does not . . . give rise to the right to deduct for tax purposes the loss of individual customers . . . [E]ach individual part enjoys no separate capital standing independent of the whole" (67-1 *USTC*, ¶9302). The names which constituted the list might fluctuate over time without necessarily diminishing the value of the asset. In a similar vein, in *Marsh & McLennan, Inc. v. Commissioner,* the court ruled that "insurance expiration" lists were nondepreciable because "first, the expirations were inextricably linked with elements of goodwill such that they had no determinable value in themselves; and second, the taxpayer had not proved that the expirations had a limited useful life, determinable with 'reasonable accuracy' "(420 *F. 2d.* 667).

In most of these cases, the deduction for depreciation for customer-based intangibles has been disallowed under Treasury *Regs* §1.167(a)(3) which provides that: "[a]n intangible asset, the useful life of which is not limited, is not subject to the allowance for depreciation . . . [and that] . . . [n]o deduction for depreciation is allowable with respect to goodwill." In cases where the taxpayer failed to convince the court that the asset had a limited useful life of an ascertainable duration, the result was a court ruling that the assets had an indefinite life. The cases rulings were not based upon customer-based intangibles being nondepreciable as a matter of law. Rather, the rulings were based upon factual characteristics; the taxpayer failed to prove a limited ascertainable useful life as required for depreciation under the *Tax Code.*

In *Houston Chronicle Publishing Co. v. U.S.,* the court clearly delineated this by stating that:

> [W]e are satisfied that the [mass asset] rule does not establish a *per se* rule of non-amortizability in every case involving both goodwill and other intangible assets. In the light of §167(a) of the Code and Regulation §1.167(a)-3, we are convinced that the "mass asset" rule does not prevent taking an amortization deduction if the taxpayer properly carries out his dual burden of proving that the intangible asset involved (1) has an ascertainable value separate and distinct from goodwill, and (2) has a limited useful life, the duration of which can be ascertained with reasonable accuracy. (73-2 *USTC* ¶9537)

The following year, in light of the *Houston Chronicle* case, the IRS issued Revenue Ruling 74-456 which modified earlier rulings to clarify that whether customer-based intangibles were distinguishable from goodwill was based upon the two-pronged test ("ascertainable value separate and distinct from goodwill" and "limited useful life") set out by the court (1974-2 *Cum. Bull.* 65, modifying *Rev. Rul.* 65-175, 1965-2 *Cum. Bull.* and *Rev. Rul.* 65-180, 1965-2 *Cum. Bull. 279*).

AFTER REV. RULING 74-456

Despite the ruling in *Houston Chronicle* and the issuance of *Rev. Rul.* 74-456, different courts continued to arrive at different decisions regarding the allowance of a depreciation deduction for customer-based intangibles. Differences have resulted from the weight placed upon each of the two prongs of the test set forth in *Houston Chronicle*. Where the focus has been on the first prong of the test, if the court has not seen the intangible as "separate and distinct from goodwill," no deduction for depreciation has been allowed. When the focus has been on the second prong, the courts have held that if the taxpayer can support a value and ascertain a limited useful life with reasonable assurance, the intangible was subject to depreciation.

CASES IN WHICH DEDUCTION WAS DISALLOWED

Following *Houston Chronicle,* when the court has disallowed a deduction, goodwill has been defined as the expectation of continued patronage, and customer-based intangibles have been seen as so inextricably linked to goodwill that they have no value "separate and distinct from goodwill." One such case was *General Television, Inc. v. U.S.*, in which the court disallowed a deduction for cable subscriber lists that were acquired as part of the purchase of cable television systems because the lists were viewed as "customer structures with the expectancy of continued patronage" and, as such, were, in essence, goodwill (77-2 *USTC* ¶9688).

In *Newark Morning Ledger Co. v. U.S.,* depreciation of purchased newspaper subscription lists containing over 460,000 names was disallowed because, even though the newspaper argued for (and the IRS "essentially" conceded that) a value and a limited useful life could be calculated for the lists, the court found that this did not sufficiently show that these intangibles were separate and distinct from goodwill (91-2 *USTC* ¶50.451). Referencing both *Commissioner v. Killian* and *Boe v. Commissioner,* the IRS argued successfully in this 1991 case that the value *Newark Morning Ledger* attached to the lists was the projected stream of income based upon the "expectation that these customers will continue their patronage"; the lists were, then, essentially a part of goodwill and, therefore, were not subject to depreciation. The court went further and delineated two possible methods for valuing intangibles—an income method and a method based on the cost of generating a similar list. When the value of the intangible is taken to be the value of the stream of income expected to be generated from the subscribers over the remaining term of their patronage (the income method), the argument that the value of the list is "separate and distinct" or different from the "expectancy of continued patronage" becomes difficult to discern. *Morning Ledger* chose to use this method and arrived at a value for the customer list of $67 million rather than a more modest $3 million value that was the government's estimated cost of generating a similar list. While the court did not state that *Morning Ledger* might have been allowed the lesser amount, it did allude to such when it stated:

> We do not decide whether *Morning Ledger* could have argued successfully that it was entitled to assign a reasonable cost basis to the list (e.g., the government's $3 million estimate of what it would cost to generate a similar list as a marketing tool) and to depreciate it as an intangible asset, notwithstanding that the list was acquired as part of a going concern. This argument has never been before the court in this case, even as an alternative claim. *Morning Ledger* apparently never has been satisfied to seek cost recovery on such a small portion of the premium it paid over the value of Booth's tangible assets. Instead, it gambled on persuading the court of the merits of its view of the definition of goodwill and the related case law in the hopes of securing the right to recover through depreciation some $67 million. In our view, however, under the proper definition of goodwill, the $67 million amount established by *Morning Ledger* is quite clearly comprised largely, if not exclusively, of amounts properly attributable to goodwill. As such, *Morning Ledger* has not satisfied its burden of proving a value for its so-called paid subscribers that is separate and distinct from goodwill. . . .

While a phalanx of cases, including *Brooks v. Commissioner* [36 *T.C.* 1128, 1133 (1961)], *Nelson Weaver Realty Co. v. Commissioner* (62-2 *USTC* ¶9719), *Skilken v. Commissioner* (70-1 *USTC* ¶9137), and *Winn-Dixie Montgomery v. U.S.* (71-1 *USTC* ¶9488), have resulted in similar rulings, not all cases have found customer-based intangibles tantamount to goodwill and denied a depreciation deduction to the taxpayer.

CASES IN WHICH A DEDUCTION WAS ALLOWED

In cases where the courts have viewed goodwill as the residual of the purchase price over the assets that can be identified (based on facts), taxpayers have found their customer-based intangibles to be depreciable assets if they have been able to show that those assets have an ascertainable value and a limited useful life that can be determined with reasonable accuracy. This deduction has been allowed even though the assets may be associated (under the law) with the "expectancy of continued patronage" in that "the old customers will resort to the old place" (*Commissioner of the Revenue v. Killian* [63-1 *USTC* ¶9347]).

As early as 1976, the courts had in some instances recognized customer-based intangibles as depreciable assets. In *Richard S. Miller & Sons, Inc. v. the United States* (76-2 *USTC* ¶9481),[3] the court found that insurance expirations had a value separate from goodwill and had a useful life that could be reasonably estimated based upon the taxpayer's experience with renewals.

In *Donrey, Inc. v. U.S.*, the 8th District Court upheld a jury verdict and found a newspaper subscription list to be a depreciable asset because it had a limited useful life and was separate and distinct from goodwill (87-1 *USTC* ¶9143). In the jury trial, Donrey had successfully argued that the subscription list it obtained as part of the purchase of the *Washington Times Herald,* a Washington, Indiana newspaper serving a farming community, had an ascertainable value of $559,406 and a useful life of twenty-three years. The trial went to extensive lengths; special interrogatories were made of the jury regarding whether the assets had an ascertainable value that was separate and distinct from goodwill and whether they had a useful life that could be determined with reasonable accuracy. Even though the jury answered the special interrogatories affirmatively, found the lists to be depreciable, and agreed with the value and life, the court noted that if it, rather than a jury, had heard the case, it would have found the lists to be nondepreciable. In hearing the case on appeal, the court affirmed the judgment of the district court and noted that the IRS had only asserted that the subscription lists were goodwill (under the law) after receiving an unfavorable verdict on the questions of whether the lists were separate and distinct from goodwill and had a limited useful life (based on the facts). Judge Bright, in dissenting, noted the similarities between this case and earlier cases (particularly *General Television Inc.*) in which the court had ruled such assets to be goodwill and, therefore, nondepreciable.[4]

A similar finding was the result in the appeal of *Emil Panichi and Emily Panichi v. United States of America* (87-2 *USTC* ¶9652). The court affirmed a lower court decision under which the taxpayer was allowed to depreciate a purchased list of trash collection customers by showing that the lists had a "discrete value, apart from goodwill" with a "depreciable life span of fifteen years and a salvage value of ten percent" (based on facts), while the government argued unsuccessfully (based on law) that the customer list was "inseparable from goodwill."

In *Colorado National Bankshares, Inc. v. Commissioner* (93-1 *USTC* ¶50,077), the taxpayer argued for the depreciation of core bank deposits obtained in the purchase of several banks. Again, the IRS argued unsuccessfully that the taxpayer was attempting to take depreciation on the expectation that these customers would continue their patronage which was, in essence, goodwill. At the same time, the taxpayer argued successfully that the core deposits had an ascertainable value and a reasonably determinable life.[5] Rather than the "expectancy of continued patronage," the court concluded that

> the value of the deposit base does not depend upon a vague hope that customers will patronize the bank for some unspecified length of time in the future. The value of the deposit base rests upon the ascertainable probability that inertia will cause depositors to leave their funds on deposit for predictable periods of time.

THE NEWARK MORNING LEDGER CASE

Clearly the courts have been divided on the issue of whether customer-based intangibles constitute goodwill. The two-pronged test used in *Houston Chronicle* did not put an end to the confusion and uncertainty. Taxpayers contemplating a purchase that included customer-based intangibles could not be certain how those assets would be viewed by the court if litigation between the taxpayer and the government resulted from depreciating those intangibles. Taxpayers who had purchased customer-based intangibles and depreciated them knew that they faced possible action by the IRS as a result of that deduction. Recently, the Supreme Court, in the 5-4 decision in *Newark Morning Ledger Co. v. United States* made strides to resolve the issue.[6]

In reversing the decision of a lower court, the Supreme Court held in *Newark* that when the taxpayer is able to prove that an asset has an ascertainable value and a limited useful life the duration of which may be determined with reasonable accuracy, the asset may be depreciated "regardless of how much the asset appears to reflect the expectancy of continued patronage." In a footnote to the opinion, the court noted that the dissenting opinions erred in suggesting "that because the 'paid subscribers' asset looks and smells like the 'expectancy of continued patronage,' it is, *ipso facto,* nondepreciable." Whether an asset is depreciable depends not on definition but on whether that asset has an ascertainable value and a limited useful life that can be determined with reasonable accuracy. The court stated that "the significant question for purposes of depreciation is not whether the asset falls 'within the core of the concept of goodwill,' . . . but whether the asset is capable of being valued and whether that value diminishes over time." This finding, the court noted, is in agreement with the government's own statement that "whether or not an intangible asset, or a tangible asset, is depreciable for Federal income tax purposes depends upon the determination that the asset is actually exhausting, and that such exhaustion is susceptible of measurement" (*Rev. Rul.* 68-483, 1968-2 *Cum. Bull.* 91-92). The fact that the lists also represented any expectation of continued patronage was "*entirely beside the point*" (emphasis added).

The court also noted that the burden of proof for the taxpayer is significant, but that the burden was eased in this particular case by the litigation strategy pursued by the IRS. The government had stipulated to the useful life assigned by the taxpayer and rested its entire case on the legal argument that the customer lists could not clearly and distinctly be distinguished from goodwill. The taxpayer, on the other hand, proved to the satisfaction of the court that the lists were not self-regenerating; they represented a "finite set that existed on a particular date." The lists were composed of identifiable subscriptions each of which had a limited useful life that could be estimated with reasonable accuracy–not of constantly fluctuating components, "merely the ebb and flow of a continuing property" (*Golden State Towel and Linen Service, Ltd. et al. v. U.S.*). When the court rejected the government's argument, "[t]his case was lost at trial."

The court went on to address the valuation of these customer-based intangibles. The court rejected the government's use of the cost approach under which the value attributed to the subscription lists was the cost of generating a similar list. Under this approach, the government assigned a value of $3 million to the paid subscribers list. The taxpayer used the "income approach" and calculated a value of $67.8 million. This represented "the present value of the after-tax subscription revenues to be derived from the 'paid subscribers,' less the cost of collecting those revenues, and adding the present value of the tax savings resulting from the depreciation of the 'paid subscribers.'" On this point the government also lost at trial by not challenging the accuracy of the $67.8 million figure. The court found that the "paid subscribers" list was more than a mere list of names and addresses and had a value in excess of such a list. The existing list represented "seasoned" subscribers. A new list would be a completely different asset; therefore, the cost of generating it would be irrelevant.

In the dissenting opinion, the justices argued that *Newark Morning Ledger* was asking the court to adopt a new definition of goodwill in which goodwill is a residual asset whose value is the "accounting leftover" of the purchase price that can not be assigned to identifiable assets that have determinable lives. The dissent returned to the argument that the paid subscribers list is the goodwill associated with those subscribers; the list is, therefore, not depreciable under the law. The dissent also questioned the method used to determine useful life and argued that *Morning Ledger* failed to show the goodwill had a useful life that was "both limited and measurable with some reasonable degree of certainty."

IMPORTANCE OF NEWARK

Prior to *Newark,* there were two distinct lines of reasoning in cases involving customer-based intangibles. When courts looked at the intangibles to determine whether they were essentially the expectation of continued patronage, these assets were generally found to be goodwill and were not depreciable under the law. When the courts looked at these intangibles in terms of the two-pronged test established in *Houston Chronicle* and the taxpayer could show to the court's satisfaction that the assets had a value separate and distinct from goodwill and a limited useful life, the assets were generally found not to be goodwill and a deduction for depreciation was allowed. The *Newark* decision rejected the first line of reasoning. Instead, if the taxpayer can meet the two-pronged test (an obstacle that is difficult, and may be impossible, to overcome), the intangibles are depreciable no matter how much they may "look, and smell, and taste" like continuing patronage. No longer need the taxpayer be concerned about which focus the court will take in these cases; the *Newark* decision concludes the conflict and confusion that had resulted from decisions of the lower courts.

Prior to *Newark* court decisions had generally allowed depreciation on customer lists purchased without purchasing the underlying assets as a going concern. For example, in *Houston Chronicle* the taxpayer purchased subscriber lists as part of the purchase of another newspaper which the taxpayer did not intend to continue publishing. Because the purchased newspaper would no longer be published, there was little question of an expectation of continuing patronage. However, in situations where lists were not purchased as free-standing assets, there has been less agreement among the courts over the question of whether the lists represent an asset distinct from goodwill or merely the expectation of continued patronage. The Supreme Court decision in *Newark* makes it clear that if the taxpayer can prove that an asset has a determinable value and a limited useful life, that asset may be depreciated "regardless of how much the asset appears to reflect the expectancy of continued patronage."

Even after *Newark,* the taxpayer still bears the burden of proving the facts concerning value and limited life, and the court indicated that this could be an awesome burden. However, the task of defending the depreciability of customer-based intangibles should be made easier by permitting the taxpayer to focus on the factual aspects of the situation rather than having attention divided between the factual aspects and making a distinction between the assets and goodwill. The court clearly pointed out that establishing value and limited life may still be too large a hurdle for the taxpayer to overcome.

REVENUE RECONCILIATION ACT OF 1993

Faced with an increasing number of cases regarding depreciation of intangibles, Congress moved to add clarification to this issue. As part of the Revenue Reconciliation Act of 1993, Congress enacted legislation that should reduce the confusion and potential litigation related to the depreciability of customer-based and certain other intangibles. Reversing the former position of the government, Section 197 requires the amortization of goodwill and certain other intangibles–such as customer-based intangibles and deposit bases of financial institutions–over a 15-year period. Now referred to as "Section 197 assets," these intangibles must have been acquired after August 10, 1993 and be "held in connection with the conduct of a trade or business" (§197 (c) (1) (B)).

This new section of the *Tax Code,* by establishing a standard useful life of 15 years for tax purposes, alleviates the difficulties that have been associated with selecting and defending methods used to determine the useful lives of these intangibles. However, because of the prospective nature of Section 197, this standard 15-year life will apply only to assets acquired after the date of enactment. Taxpayers who acquired this type of asset prior to that date still need to be prepared to defend the useful lives that they have used in computing depreciation.

CONCLUSION

Faced with the Supreme Court decision in *Newark* and the addition of Section 197 to the *Tax Code,* the IRS would be expected to become more aggressive in disputing the value of the assets. *Newark* removed the issue of the expectation of continued patronage automatically making an asset nondepreciable; Section 197 establishes a standard 15-year life for income tax purposes for acquisitions after August 10, 1993. Taxpayers with assets acquired before the enactment of Section 197 will still be required to meet the second prong of the fact test and establish a limited useful life. The issue remaining for all taxpayers is the determination of the value of their customer-based intangibles, and taxpayers should be ready to defend their valuation methods. Here again, however, *Newark* has offered guidance in rejecting the government's cost approach in favor of the taxpayer's income approach.

Newark and Section 197 have brought light to an area that has been fraught with uncertainty for taxpayers. Now, through careful planning at the time of acquisition, the taxpayer should be more certain of being able to obtain depreciation deductions that might not have been available in the past. The burden of proof will still be upon the taxpayer to prove the facts in the case, especially valuation, but the task should be easier with the removal of two earlier areas of dispute.

NOTES

1. "Depreciation" is used for tangible assets while "amortization" is used for intangible assets. However, in the Tax Code, in judicial decisions, and in general usage, depreciation frequently is used to cover both "depreciation" and "amortization." A third category, "depletion," is used for natural resources.

2. Kieso, D. E. and Weygandt, J.J., *Intermediate Accounting: Seventh Edition,* p. 543.

3. The full title of the case is *Richard S. Miller & Sons, Inc., Richard S. Miller and Edith V. Miller, Douglass W. Miller and Joyce M. Miller, and Daniel Miller and Janis R. Miller v. The United States* (76-2 *USTC* ¶9481).

4. Contrast this with the earlier cited cases and cases such as *Golden State Towel and Linen Service, Ltd. and Oakland California Towel Company v. The United States* (67-1 *USTC* par. 9302) in which customer lists were found not to be depreciable and a deduction for a loss was allowed for tax purposes only in the year in which "all or a substantial identifiable, vendible portion of the list was terminated permanently and then only where the loss could be adequately measured."

5. Contrast this outcome with *AmSouth Bancorporation and Subsidiaries v. United States of America* (88-1 *USTC* par. 9232) in which the taxpayer was denied a deduction for the depreciation of customer base deposit when the court felt that the taxpayer had "not met its burden of proving that the customer deposit base had a value which was separate and distinct from the goodwill." The court went further to state:

> At the possible risk of being too simplistic, the court would make the following observation. When deposits are made, two accounting entries result. First, there is a debit (asset) entry for cash or its equivalent. Second, there is an equal and offsetting credit (liability) entry for the liability to the depositor. Any additional asset must be different from the cash thereby acquired. Its creation must, somehow, result from the expectation that the depositor will allow the cash, or its equivalent, to remain as an asset and that earnings will result therefrom. This expectation is akin to, if not tantamount, to the expectancy that 'old customers will resort to the old place' of business or *continued* 'customer patronage'. The 'additional' asset does not just materialize out of nowhere. It is geared to the expectancy of the continued deposit relationship (patronage).

6. *Newark Morning Ledger Co. v. United States*, 91-2 *USTC* para.50,451, 945 *F.2d* 555, rev'g and rem'g 90-1 *USTC* para 50,193 (DC-N.J.), 734 *F.Supp.* 176.

7. This was the date of enactment of Section 197.

FAIR USE

Free Ride or Fair Use: An Analysis of *American Geophysical Union v. Texaco, Inc.*

Todd S. Parkhurst

For-profit businesses that regularly circulate publications to employees for photocopying of significant articles should closely examine the influential Second Circuit Court of Appeals' recent decision in *American Geophysical Union v. Texaco, Inc.*[1] American Geophysical Union and eighty other publishers of scientific and technical journals filed the lawsuit claiming that unauthorized photocopying of journal articles by Texaco constituted copyright infringement. The parties agreed to narrow the scope of the trial to whether photocopying of one journal's articles by a randomly selected Texaco researcher was a "fair use" within the meaning of Section 107 of the Copyright Act.[2] The court concluded that making such

---

Todd S. Parkhurst, Esq. is a partner in Gardner, Carton & Douglas, 321 N. Clark Street, Chicago, IL 60610.

The author acknowledges with appreciation the editorial assistance provided by Jennifer Cervan.

[Haworth co-indexing entry note]: "Free Ride or Fair Use: An Analysis of *American Geophysical Union v. Texaco, Inc.*" Parkhurst, Todd S. Co-published simultaneously in *The Acquisitions Librarian* (The Haworth Press, Inc.) No. 15, 1996, pp. 61-67; and: *Current Legal Issues in Publishing* (ed: A. Bruce Strauch) The Haworth Press, Inc., 1996, pp. 61-67. Single or multiple copies of this article are available from The Haworth Document Delivery Service [1-800-342-9678, 9:00 a.m. - 5:00 p.m. (EST)].

photocopies and placing them in files for the purpose of faciliating future research–or "archival" photocopying–is a copyright violation. Because the researcher essentially was creating his own library at the expense of the publisher, the fair use defense did not apply. Given the substanial damages that courts can award for copyright infringement,[3] the ruling has been called "a significant victory for publishers"[4] and for the Copyright Clearance Center, which licenses photocopying of articles from one-third of the world's scientific journals.[5]

Because the *Texaco* decision was restricted to whether the photocopying was a fair use within the meaning of Section 107, the court did not address the applicability of Section 108 of the Copyright Act. Section 108 permits qualifying libraries to make single photocopies of articles for researchers if the copies are made "without any purpose of direct or indirect commercial advantage." One of the requirements for the Section 108 exemption is that a library must be publicly operated or open to outside researchers, a definition which would exclude the in-house libraries of most corporations and law firms, which usually do not open their collections to outsiders. However, if the photocopying activity does not fall within the Section 108 exemption, the library may still use the fair use defense from Section 107.

The *Texaco* case has set authors and other copyright owners, who favor the result, against librarians and for-profit research-oriented companies, who oppose it. In their brief to the Second Circuit, the plaintiff publishers stated that companies like Texaco that routinely photocopy articles for research purposes are merely attempting to take a "free ride" by obtaining valuable intellectual property rights without paying for them. "If everybody is copying and no one is supporting the production of original materials, there won't be any original materials at some point," said American Geophysical Union spokesperson Judy Holoviak.[6]

On the other hand, as the American Library Association pointed out in an amicus brief supporting Texaco's position, photocopying is essential for libraries whose role is to disseminate knowledge. According to the ALA, if photocopying journal articles is not a fair use, libraries will either "be required to succumb to the unregulated royalty structure designed and imposed by the [CCC] or to assume the burden of ascertaining the employment status and intent of every library user who wishes to make a copy, as well as the ultimate purpose to which the copy would be put."

The court of appeals emphasized that its ruling in *Texaco* is limited to the particular circumstances of the case. Those circumstances, however, are fairly common. The researcher selected to represent all Texaco employees, Dr. Donald H. Chickering II, is a chemical engineer employed at a Texaco research facility. Like many researchers, Chickering placed his name on routing lists of scientific and technical journals and regularly photocopied or instructed Texaco's library to photocopy in their entirety articles he believed would be useful to him in current or future research. He typically did not use the photocopied articles immediately but rather retained them in his files for future reference.

Chickering's files contained twenty-five photocopies of articles published by plaintiff Academic Press, Inc. in the *Journal of Catalysis,* a monthly publication that reports research data and studies on catalysis, which concerns changes in the rates of chemical reactions.[7] Photocopies of eight of those *Catalysis* articles were selected as the exemplars for purposes of the fair use trial. Texaco had purchased several institutional and individual subscriptions to *Catalysis.*[8] Academic Press also offered bound annual volumes of back issues, reprints, and authorization to photocopy articles from *Catalysis* through the CCC.

The CCC offers two licensing systems through which users can obtain advance authorization to photocopy copyrighted articles from registered publications. The Annual Authorization Service (AAS) grants the user a blanket annual license to make an unlimited number of photocopies from registered publications for internal use. The annual AAS license fee is based on several factors, including an on-site photocopying survey, licensing fees charged by the journals that are regularly copied by the user or similar users, and the user's employee population. The CCC also offers a Transactional Reporting Service (TRS), which provides for blanket advance permission to copy registered publications provided that the user subsequently reports the photocopying to the CCC and pays the appropriate fees that the copyright owners of the copied articles have established. The TRS option requires users to maintain logs of every copy made.[9]

Texaco argued that Chickering's photocopying was a fair use, as codified in Section 107 of the Copyright Act, and that therefore his action did not constitute copyright infringement. In determining whether the fair use defense applied, the court analyzed the four non-exclusive fair use factors set forth in Section 107: (1) the purpose and character of the use; (2) the nature of the copyrighted work; (3) the amount and substantiality of the portion used in relation to the copyrighted work as a whole; and (4) the effect of the use on the potential market for or the value of the copyrighted work. The court held that all but the second factor favored the publishers; thus, the fair use defense did not apply.

With respect to the first factor–the purpose and character of the use–the court characterized Chickering's photocopying as " 'archival'–i.e., done for the primary purpose of providing Chickering with his own personal copy of each article without Texaco's having to purchase another original journal."[10] Chickering primarily was creating a personal office file of potentially useful articles for future use rather than making copies for immediate use in a laboratory experiment. Such photocopying "merely supersedes the objects of the original creation,"[11] and is not "transformative" in nature (i.e., it did not add anything "new" to the original work).[12] Therefore, the court concluded that the first factor favored the publishers, "primarily because the dominant purpose of the use is archival–to assemble a set of papers for future reference, thereby serving the same purpose for which additional subscriptions are normally sold, or for which photocopying licenses may be obtained."[13]

The court considered the second factor–the nature of the work–to favor Texaco because the photocopied articles were "essentially factual in nature and the 'scope of fair use is greater with respect to factual than nonfactual works'."[14] Conversely, the court determined that the third factor–the amount and substantiality of the portion of the copyrighted work used–clearly favored the publishers because Chickering copied the eight articles from *Catalysis* in their entirety.

In analyzing the fourth statutory fair use factor–the effect of the use on the copyrighted works' potential market or value–the court found that unauthorized photocopying could have a significant effect on the publishers in the form of lost licensing and subscription revenues. Texaco had obtained permission to photocopy directly from publishers, purchased additional subscriptions to various publications, and purchased photocopies from document delivery services. Accordingly, if employees required additional copies, Texaco had the option to use existing licensing schemes or purchase additional subscriptions for each of its researchers who wished to keep issues of *Catalysis* on the office shelf. Thus, the court concluded that the fourth statutory factor favored the publishers. The court explicitly rejected the dissenting judge's opinion that the market for licensing photocopies is insufficiently developed to be considered in weighing market harm.

The *Texaco* decision is likely to become a key precedent regarding photocopying and fair use over the next several years. It is difficult, however, to predict the precise impact the case will have beyond the strictures it places on for-profit companies that photocopy articles for archival research purposes. While the *Texaco* decision will undoubtedly affect photocopying and licensing practices, just how far it will extend to other settings remains to be seen.[15]

Clearly, the routine, systematic, and wholesale photocopying of journal articles for archival research purposes in profit-making enterprises will be considered copyright infringement, unless the institution pays a proper royalty or licensing fee. Therefore, in the wake of *Texaco,* prudent companies will police the photocopying habits of their employees, educate their workers on copyright compliance, and consider the purchase of additional subscriptions to frequently used journals or the licensing of photocopies through an organization such as the Copyright Clearance Center.

However, the *Texaco* decision should not be interpreted expansively as a far-reaching attempt to curtail all photocopying, some of which remains protected by fair use under Section 107 of the Copyright Act or the special provision for copying by libraries under Section 108. The *Texaco* court acknowledged that under the Act, some types of copying are considered fair use, but the court held that the specific copying in question did not meet the applicable standard. Therefore, under different facts, fair use may apply. For example, if a researcher makes an abstract of an article and files that abstract for future reference, that could be considered a "transformative" use that is likely to be protected. Or, if only small portions of an article or journal are archived in a personal file, to aid in later retrieval of the full text from the institution's in-house library when needed, that, too, may be allowed under the principle of fair use. Similarly, the photocopying of a journal's table of contents may be an acceptably insubstantial portion of the whole to fall under fair use.

Because the *Texaco* case focused solely on researchers at money-making companies, the question remains open as to how a court would view similiar acts by researchers at educational institutions who do consulting work under grants from profit-making enterprises. For example, if Professor Joe Smith, at a large Midwestern research university, receives a research grant from a Big Three automaker to develop a more efficient engine, would the professor's photocopying activities for that project be considered a fair use? The answer remains to be seen.

Furthermore, it is important to note that ideas and facts themselves are not subject to copyright protection–copyright protects the medium of expression of the ideas, not the ideas themselves. Thus, for example, a researcher might be able to copy down a scientific formula or a particular statistical calculation for use in research without fear of copyright infringement.

The bottom line is that, in this information age, courts will continue to be called upon to strike a balance between the copyright holder's economic interests and society's interest in access to information. If nothing else, the *Texaco* decision sounded a warning to consumers of information, who now must be not just cognizant of copyright issues, but vigilant in their compliance with the law.

NOTES

1. 37 F.3d 881 (2nd Cir. 1994).

2. Fair use, as defined in Section 107 of the Copyright Act, is an affirmative defense to a claim of copyright infringement. Section 107 provides, in pertinent part:

> . . . . [T]he fair use of a copyrighted work, including such use by reproduction in copies or phonorecords or by any other means specified by that section, for purposes such as criticism, comment, news reporting, teaching (including multiple copies for classroom use), scholarship, or research, is not an infringement of copyright. In determining whether the use made of a work in any particular case is a fair use the factors to be considered shall include:
>
> (1) the purpose and character of the use, including whether such use is of commercial nature or is for nonprofit educational purposes;
> (2) the nature of the copyrighted work;
> (3) the amount and substantiality of the portion used in relation to the copyrighted work as a whole; and
> (4) the effect of the use upon the potential market for or value of the copyrighted work. 17 U.S.C. § 107.

3. The Copyright Act permits prevailing plaintiffs to recover either statutory damages, which can range from $500 to $20,000 per infringement, or actual damages plus the infringer's profits, 17 U.S.C. § 504(c). If the infringement was "willful," the court may award up to $100,000 per infringement. In addition, the infringer may be liable for the plaintiff's costs and attorney fees, 17 U.S.C. § 505.

4. Martin Flumenbaum, Brad S. Karp, "The Doctrine of Fair Use," N.Y.L.J., Nov. 23, 1994.

5. The CCC is "a non-profit, central clearinghouse established in 1977 by publishers, authors and photocopy users" which was "formed in response to a Congressional recommendation that an efficient mechanism be established to license photocopying," *American Geophysical Union v. Texaco, Inc.*, 802 F. Supp. 1, 7 (S.D.N.Y. 1992). Thus, the CCC was established after the decision in *Williams & Wilkins Co. v. United States,* 487 F.2d 1345 (Ct. Cl. 1973), *aff'd,* 420 U.S. 376 (1975), which held that photocopying done by employees of the National Institute of Health qualified for fair use protection because it served to advance science. The district court in *Texaco* concluded that new photocopying licensing mechanisms, exemplified by the CCC, were a "monumental change," 802 F. Supp. at 24. Therefore, unlike the defendant in *Williams & Wilkins,* "Texaco could conveniently, and without undue administrative burden, retain the benefits of photocopying at will, simply by complying with one of CCC's licensing systems," *Id.* at 25.

6. Alex Philippidis, "Texaco Appeals 'Fair Use' Ruling in Copyright Suit," Westchester County Bus. J., Nov. 28, 1994, 1.

7. Authors whose articles appear in *Catalysis,* who are not paid for their writing, must assign their copyrights in published articles to Academic Press, 37 F.3d at 884.

8. Since 1988, Texaco had maintained three subscriptions to *Catalysis.* Academic Press offered two types of subscriptions to *Catalysis,* an institutional rate, which was $828 a year at the relevant time, and an individual rate, which was approximately half the institutional rate, or about $424, 802 F. Supp. 1, 7.

9. As of January 1991, about 400 users reported to the CCC under the TRS method, and more than 100 corporate licensees reported under the AAS method, 802 F. Supp. at 8.

10. 37 F.3d at 888.

11. *Id.* at 888 (quoting *Campbell v. Acuff Rose Music, Inc.*, 114 S.Ct. 1164, 1171 (1994)).

12. The dissenting judge, on the other hand, felt that the purpose of Chickering's photocopying was transformative, equating it with note-taking as part of the creative research process. 37 F. 3d at 900-901 (Jacobs, dissenting).

13. 37 F.3d at 892.

14. *Id.* at 893 (quoting 802 F. Supp. at 16-17).

15. Texaco's attorney, Richard DeSevo, has expressed concern that "[t]he rationale for the decision could ultimately be applied to professional people other than scientists, such as lawyers, doctors, judges and journalists." Philippidis, Westchester County Bus. J., Nov. 28, 1994, 1. Others feel that while the *Texaco* ruling might not cause individuals and small businesses to alter their photocopying habits, "large companies with deep pockets will be in for a rude and costly shock." James Evans, *The Los Angeles Times*, Nov. 30, 1994, 10.

Universities, Libraries and Fair Use in the Digital Age

Laura N. Gasaway

INTRODUCTION

The arrival of the digital age has been heralded as the most significant change in the distribution of information since the invention of the printing press. As universities and libraries enter the electronic age, copyrighted print works have not disappeared. Instead, institutions find that they must support research, teaching and learning with both the print and electronic materials. For the most part, the current Copyright Act[1] has worked well for universities and libraries because of the special exemptions that exist for these institutions. Libraries are permitted to make single copies of copyrighted works, such as journal articles, for users who need them for scholarship, research or teaching; libraries can even obtain reproductions of copies of works for users from other libraries through interlibrary loan. Teaching is facilitated through the broad classroom exemption for face-to-face teaching in nonprofit educational institutions, and, to a lesser degree, by the narrow exemption for instructional broadcasting. Despite these exemptions, librarians, faculty members and administrators have suggested some amendments to the law to facilitate the use of audiovisual works in education and for distance learning situations and to permit faculty creation and use of multimedia works without having to obtain prior permission from copyright holders to incorporate small portions of

---

Laura N. Gasaway is Director of the Law Library, Professor of Law at the University of North Carolina and past president of the American Association of Law Libraries.

[Haworth co-indexing entry note]: "Universities, Libraries and Fair Use in the Digital Age." Gasaway, Laura N. Co-published simultaneously in *The Acquisitions Librarian* (The Haworth Press, Inc.) No. 15, 1996, pp. 69-87; and: *Current Legal Issues in Publishing* (ed: A. Bruce Strauch) The Haworth Press, Inc., 1996, pp. 69-87. Single or multiple copies of this article are available from The Haworth Document Delivery Service [1-800-342-9678, 9:00 a.m. - 5:00 p.m. (EST)].

copyrighted materials in multimedia works the faculty member creates to use in his or her class. Further, universities and their libraries want to be able to use technology to exercise the exemptions afforded them under the Act. They want to substitute electronic reserve collections for traditional photocopy collections, to digitize collections of slides to enhance research and the use of these valuable research tools, to allow library users to browse electronic works, and to preserve deteriorating printed materials, audiovisual works, software and electronic works using available technological means.

Despite some claims that copyright protections will be unnecessary in the digital age because licensing schemes can be implemented to govern access issues, many scholars and other experts continue to believe such protection is not only necessary but desirable. To these parties, copyright protection is essential in the electronic environment if publishers and producers of copyrighted works are to make their works available in digital format. The owners of works must have the ability to control the distribution of works and to ensure their integrity before copyright holders will risk the capital required to make works available electronically. As the report entitled *Intellectual Property and the National Information Infrastructure: A Preliminary Draft of the Report of the Working Group on Intellectual Property Rights (i.e., the Green Paper)*[2] stated:

> The intellectual property regime must recognize the legitimate rights and commercial expectations of owners of the works used in the National Information Infrastructure environment, whether the work is used with or without their permission and ensure that users have access to the broadest feasible variety of works on terms and conditions that promote the progress of science and the useful arts.[2]

Although copyright originally was developed for printed works, it can be expanded to encompass the new digital environment as well with some amendments to the statute and some expansion of existing definitions. While both users of copyrighted works and copyright holders may agree that changes are needed, what shape these alterations should take enjoys no broad agreement.

Thus, the challenge for universities and libraries is to work diligently to ensure that their interests are represented in the legislative arena and that any changes extend fair use to the electronic environment. At the same time, representatives of university and library organizations must work with representatives of the copyright holder community to develop guidelines and understandings that meet the needs of both groups. The changing nature of the environment in which works are increasingly available in electronic format presents yet another challenge. Neither copyright owners nor the university and library communities can predict with certainty how the digital environment will develop. Thus, there is some fear on both sides that changes proposed may later prove to be detrimental rather than helpful. These two groups, which may be characterized as the creator and user communities, cannot exist without each other. Continued dialog between the groups is essential. Staking out inalterable positions is counterproductive if the debate is to continue. Because of the instability of the environment, both sides of the debate must remain flexible and recognize the genuine interests of the other side.

GENERAL MATTERS

Section 102 of the Copyright Act generally provides that original works of authorship fixed in tangible media of expression are eligible for copyright protection. The statute then lists eight categories of works for which copyright protection is available.[3] Even some of these basic concepts cause difficulties in the electronic environment. For example, only *original* works are eligible for copyright protection; and, embodied in the originality requirement, is a standard of at least minimal creativity.[4] Many extremely useful compilations of data may lack sufficient originality to qualify for copyright protection. Likewise, the fixation requirement causes some difficulties in the digital age. Fixation means that a work must be "fixed in tangible media of expression, now known or later developed."[5] If a digital work is stored on a CD-ROM or on tape or disk, clearly it is fixed. There is some debate, however, about whether a work that exists only in RAM is fixed; the weight of authority appears to be that such work is fixed for copyright purposes.[6]

Concepts such as authorship and ownership also are less clear in the electronic environment. For example, who is the author when many individuals contribute to a discussion on a listserv or other interactive work? At what point is the authorship settled and final? Likewise, ownership of the work is less clear. Who owns the copyright in these works? As the electronic world evolves, many of these questions will be answered by Congress and the courts, but it is not likely that the answers to these questions will come without acrimony.

The copyright statute details the five rights of the copyright holder: reproduction, distribution, adaptation, performance and display.[7] Each of the five rights is implicated in library and educational uses of copyrighted digital works. For example, is the work reproduced every time it is read on the screen? If a library subscribes to an electronic work, may portions of the work be printed or downloaded for or by library users and students? Are students permitted to adapt digital copyrighted works as a learning exercise? May faculty members scan a work and then project the digitized image to a class? When a work such as a videotape is retrieved and played on a laptop computer in a public place (such as an airport terminal), is it a public performance such that public performance rights are triggered? What about displays in such places? So, even fairly well settled concepts such as the rights of the copyright owner are not so clear in the digital world. These and other questions along with rapidly changing technology create an unstable environment for both copyright holders and for universities, libraries and their users.

FAIR USE

The primary concern for libraries and educational institutions is to ensure that students, faculty, staff and researchers be able to use digital works in the same manner as they are currently permitted to use printed works. For teaching activities, extension of fair use to the digital world means the ability to use electronic works in the classroom just as if they were traditional works, to extend the classroom exemption to include distance learning, to create and use multimedia works in the classroom, and to digitize existing slide collections for classroom and research use. This means extension of the fair use privilege to electronic works and to permit the §108 exempted libraries activities to be conducted using the available technology. Such uses likely would include the right to browse electronic works, to preserve works using electronic methods, to make electronic copies of printed works for users under the same conditions detailed in § 108(d)-(e), to create and use electronic reserve collections, and to conduct interlibrary loan activities within the Interlibrary Loan Guidelines[8] but through electronic means.

Fair use is both a limitation on the exclusive rights of the copyright holder and a defense to copyright infringement. Fair use excuses conduct which otherwise would be infringement.

> . . . The fair use of a copyrighted work, including such use by reproduction in copies or phonorecords or by any other means specified by that section, for purposes such as criticism, comment, news reporting, teaching (including multiple copies for classroom use), scholarship, or research is not an infringement of copyright.[9]

The statute then lists four factors that courts are to consider when evaluating a use to determine if it is a fair use: (1) *Purpose and character of the use* considers whether the use is for scholarship or commercial gain, whether the use is a transformative use or a productive use. (2) *Nature of the copyrighted work* requires an examination of the characteristics of the copyrighted work itself. (3) *Amount and substantiality used in comparison to the work as a whole* is both a quantitative and a qualitative test, but there is no bright line quantitative standard that can be used to determine whether a use is fair. (4) *Effect on the market for or value of the work* looks at the economic impact of the use on the copyright holder. The Classroom Guidelines[10] were negotiated during the copyright law revision process, and they provide a safe harbor for teachers in nonprofit educational institutions who need to reproduce copyrighted works for their students. There are several tests such as brevity, spontaneity, cumulative effects and notice of copyright that must be met in order for a teacher to take advantage of the guidelines. Although they are minimum and not maximum guidelines, and while many faculty find them to be overly restrictive, these guidelines have provided some certainty for permissible copying activity in the course of instruction since they contain specific quantitative standards.

The Classroom Guidelines do not permit the creation of coursepacks by faculty members without permission of the copyright holder. In *Basic Books, Inc. v. Kinko's Graphics Corp.*,[11] the district court discussed the guidelines in the context of a commercial copying service that reproduced book chapters, journal articles, and the like, assembled them into coursepacks and sold them to students. Even though the coursepacks were produced at the request of individual faculty members and were used as teaching materials, the court held that while the materials would ultimately be used for nonprofit educational purposes, the Classroom Guidelines were not available to a commercial copy service.[12] The case also may be read as giving a fairly strong endorsement to the guidelines.

Not only must fair use be preserved in the digital environment, but teachers and librarians must be able to use technological means to meet their teaching, research and service obligations while still preserving the rights of the copyright holders and complying with the spirit of the copyright law. Students in nonprofit educational institutions must be allowed to use copyrighted works in electronic format to enhance their learning just as they can use printed works today.

UNIVERSITY TEACHING AND THE DIGITAL ENVIRONMENT

Educational institutions must be able to reproduce digital works for students under similar conditions as those detailed in the Classroom Guidelines. The Green Paper states that "Like the library exemptions, the educational use exemptions are provided in addition to the fair use. Thus, general fair use should cover such uses, and other general exemptions, which are also available to educational institutions."[13] Reproduction of a copyrighted work for educational uses might be in the form of printouts from the digital work or they might simply be downloaded copies of the work for each student in the class. The reproductions also might take the form of digitized copies of printed works.

Classroom Exemption

One of the broadest and most important limitations on the exclusive rights of the copyright owner for educational institutions is the § 110(1) so-called classroom exemption. The Copyright Act states that "performance or display of a work by instructors or pupils in the course of face-to-face teaching activities of a nonprofit educational institution, in a classroom, or other similar place devoted to instruction" is permitted.[14] All works are covered so that a teacher may read aloud from a copyrighted work, play a copyrighted videotape, display a slide or transparency, so long as the copy of the audiovisual work or display of individual images is a lawfully made copy.[15] There should be little difficulty in expanding the limitation to permit the performance or display of digital works in the course of instruction. The current law permits a teacher to use an opaque projector to project an image so that the display may be seen by students. Many experts argue that the making of transparencies and slides also are permitted for the classroom. Does the use of a digital camera to display a work involve making a copy? If so, is this copy one that is considered to be lawfully made under § 110(1)? Suppose that the faculty member scans the image and stores it in a computer and then displays it using an LCD panel. Is this functionally different from using an opaque projector or making a transparency? Even if it is, should the use be permitted under fair use or under an expanded view of § 110(1)?

The reason the classroom exemption exists is to further a student's education by permitting teachers or students to display or perform works in the course of instruction without having to obtain permission of the copyright holder. Public policy dictates that this be extended to electronic works.

Multimedia

One current difficulty for faculty is the creation of multimedia works for instruction. When the faculty member creates a multimedia work, he or she typically reproduces copyrighted works or portions of such works by incorporating them into a multimedia work. These may include text, graphics, photographs, music and video or film clips. Presumably the performance or display of the multimedia work in the classroom would be permitted under § 110(1); it is the reproduction of copyrighted works that is the problem. Under the current law, in order to create such works, the faculty member would have to seek permission from each copyright holder, a daunting task indeed. Faculty posit that inclusion of portions of copyrighted materials in a multimedia work to be used solely in the classroom should be allowed since the performance and display is permitted under § 110(1). The use of technology to reproduce, combine and store the work should not change the underlying policy, i.e., to permit performances and displays of copyrighted works for classroom instruction in nonprofit educational institutions.

The interests of the various components of the copyright holder community are not the same, and there are no blanket rights or even blanket rights permissions organizations for all types of works. There are some stock photography companies which can provide blanket rights and there are CD-ROM's with royalty cleared high-resolution photographs that can be incorporated into multimedia works.[16] Additionally, there are compact disks of recorded music in which the rights have been cleared to use for multimedia works for the classroom. There also are some royalty-free videoclips which can be purchased for use in multimedia works. Inclusion of other videoclips in a multimedia work, however, requires the permission of the copyright holder and often a fee is charged for even a single use. Any of these works a teacher wants to incorporate into a multimedia work may be available in digital format, and the need to include them is not different from the need to include current works available in print, graphics, sound recordings or audiovisual works in faculty-created multimedia works for classroom use.

Faculty seek the right to prepare multimedia works for the classroom without having to obtain prior permission from copyright holders. It is virtually impossible to obtain the permissions for occasional use. It is difficult because of the number of copyright holders that would have to be contacted and because of the time element. Today's students demand current material more than ever before, and faculty will want to update these multimedia works regularly, so seeking permission would become an on-going task. Certainly, a time limit on the use of multimedia works created by faculty for use in their classrooms is reasonable, such as two years.[17] After that time, for continued use, permission could be required. Faculty members maintain that combining works electronically should be no different if the works are individually owned by the school and use will be limited to the classroom. The situation changes, however, when the multimedia work becomes shared by several faculty members or widely distributed, even if that distribution is free of charge. In this latter instance, clearly permissions would have to be sought and royalties paid if requested by the individual copyright owners.

It also should be noted that students will want to create multimedia works for class projects or as theses and dissertations. When these works are to be used in a nonprofit school in face-to-face teaching, the students should be allowed to create and use these works just as faculty should be able to do. Thus, the problem may be somewhat broader than just faculty-created works.

Distance Learning

Increasingly, educational institutions are recognizing distance learning as the growth area for higher education. In a college or university, basic instruction might be delivered to remote locations on the campus such as dormitory rooms; it also could be delivered to sites physically remote from the campus. Participation in distance learning courses already is occurring from community colleges to research universities and includes a variety of subjects and disciplines including professional education courses in medicine, nursing and law.

Congress considered the possibility of distance learning when it enacted the Copyright Act of 1976. Section 110(2) deals with instructional broadcasting, but its very narrowness demonstrates the development stage of distance education in 1976 rather than the present reality. The Act permits the transmission of copyrighted works in the course of instruction in nonprofit educational institutions and government entities. Transmissions are restricted by type of work included, where the reception may occur and by purpose of the broadcast. Only nondramatic literary works and musical works may be used in instructional broadcasting according to the statute. The performance or display that will be broadcast must be of material assistance to the teaching content of the course. Further, the transmission must be received in a classroom or similar place devoted to instruction. Reception for disabled persons unable to attend a regular classroom also is allowed.[18]

Educational institutions seek to have this section of the Act amended for a variety of reasons all related to modern distance learning. Instructors use a variety of materials in teaching, not just nondramatic literary and musical works. Prime among these are audiovisual works, and especially videotapes. Increasingly, multimedia works will be used as these become available for the education market. If a teacher is permitted to perform a copyrighted videotape in her class when face-to-face teaching is involved, should students enrolled in the class for distance learning be restricted in what they are permitted to view? Not only does this unduly restrict teaching but also learning. Faculty members want to be able to teach the same class in the same way regardless of whether the student is physically located at the campus where the course is being taught or whether the student is taking the course via distance learning. Laws should make sense, and faculty members often fail to see the logic that permits use of videotapes in their classrooms but not for distance learning when it is the very same course that is being delivered. Not just the same content, but the identical course. Further, these courses are increasingly interactive and are offered through video conferencing and the like. Why should the face-to-face requirement not extend to distance learners, especially those involved in interactive instruction?

There is little faculty complaint about the restriction that the transmission of the copyrighted work must be of material assistance to the teaching content of the class. This provision likely was inserted to differentiate performances of works for entertainment as opposed to performances in the course of instruction. Entertainment traditionally is a performance for which royalties are paid. Indeed, movie studios such as Disney Studios now offer annual licenses to schools for the performances of copyrighted works for entertainment purposes. Thus, schools or day care centers that want to use performances of these works for rewards for students or for entertainment may do so upon payment of royalty fees or by taking an annual license. But, does the requirement that the performance or display be of material assistance to the teaching content of the class permit the use of background music in an educational broadcast?

Another restriction in § 110(2) is that reception must be in a classroom or other location where instruction normally occurs. While many distance learning students do sit in distance classrooms and receive the course as transmitted, increasingly, students will receive the transmission in their workplaces or in their homes. Why does it matter where the instruction takes place as long as the course is offered by a nonprofit educational institution? Certainly, it is logical to restrict reception to persons formally enrolled in the course. But if students are formally enrolled and if the course is the same course taught to students on the campus, does it make sense to treat distance learning differently?

Digitization of Slides

Another important issue for universities and libraries is the interest in digitizing slide collections to improve access to these slides, to better organize the collections and to facilitate their use in the classroom and in research. Many of the slide collections consist of art or architectural images and are used by faculty to illustrate their lectures and by students for study and research purposes. Other large slide collections are made up of medical, botanical and other scientific slides. Over the years both individual faculty members and libraries have built considerable collections of slides to be used to illustrate their lectures. Many of these slides were purchased, but others have been made from photographs published in books. Additionally, these slide collections contain original slides taken by faculty members. Many of these images contain no information concerning copyright ownership, although those that are available commercially tend to contain the notice of copyright when they are sold. In an effort to save space or to integrate a variety of slides, many slide collection curators over the years removed slides from their cardboard casings, thus losing any copyright notice or other information about copyright ownership. Both faculty and libraries have tended to mix slides from these various sources and have arranged them by subject or other theme to facilitate teaching. This means that when the curator or a user views the slide, he or she generally does not know whether the image was purchased, produced as an original work by a faculty member or reproduced from a printed publication.

It should be stated that the Copyright Act permits one to hold copyright in a photograph, i.e., a slide, even though that slide is a photograph of a public domain work. The slide has its own originality as a photograph.[19] Thus, for copyright purposes, when one speaks of copyright in an image, it is the copyright in the photograph or slide that is relevant and not the copyright status of the underlying painting or sculpture. Of course, the underlying art object also may be separately copyrighted, but frequently they are in the public domain.

Preservation of these slide collections is of considerable concern to universities and libraries, and current technology permits one to scan these images and to create a database of the slides. The database then can be searched either in the library on a dedicated terminal or from any terminal if the database is made available via the campus network. Further, a user then could print an image or download it to disk for subsequent use.

There are a number of pilot projects dealing with the digitization of slide collections, especially those at the Smithsonian and at various museums. These institutions own the copyright in the slides they are digitizing. The libraries and faculty members who want to digitize university slide collections must recognize that the school typically does not own the copyright in the photograph. What it may own is the only copy of the photograph, however. Some of the photographs/slides may be in the public domain, but in all likelihood, neither the library nor the faculty member knows the copyright status of the individual image. The reasons academic institutions want to digitize their slide collections include: (1) for preservation purposes, (2) to save space, (3) to increase access, (4) to facilitate display of the slides in the classroom, (5) to create reserve collections of slides for students so they can access them repeatedly during the semester, and (6) to improve the indexing of the slide collections and the ability of researchers to access the slides.

There are two types of digitization projects which may dictate different answers to the questions copyright poses. The first type of slide digitization is one that creates low-resolution, thumbnail sized images which merely assists the user in identifying that a slide exists. In other words, such a database would serve as a finding tool only. Presumably, reproduction from these low-resolution images would be unlikely; even using these images for class demonstration purposes would be of limited value. The primary use for these digitized images is to create a better catalog, provide additional subject access to the slides and thus to enhance use of the collection. Presumably, a teacher would use the database to determine that the slide collection contains a particular image. Then he or she would retrieve the slide to use for display to a class.

The second type of project combines the low-resolution, thumbnail photographic images for identification and access with high-resolution reuse capability. Thus, a user could enlarge the photograph and display it from the database or could print or download the image for use to display in classes (without going back to the original slide). Additionally a user might be able to use the image and incorporate it in a subsequent multimedia work or other publication.

Clearly, both types of digitization are reproductions. For those slides that are copyrighted and those that were made by faculty members, the question is whether the activity constitutes fair use when the use of the database of digitized images is within a nonprofit educational institution and is used for teaching, scholarship and research. It is fairly easy to make an argument that the thumbnail sized, low-resolution image is a fair use since its use is to facilitate use of the regular slide itself. It is somewhat more difficult to argue fair use for databases of images that incorporate high-resolution digitized images which themselves may be displayed directly from the database, printed and perhaps even reused in subsequent works such as multimedia or printed publications. Some institutions are proceeding with projects to digitize their slide collections, however, and will not restrict the use. They simply have determined that the risk of being sued for copyright infringement is low.

LIBRARIES AND DIGITAL WORKS

Libraries operate relatively well under the 1976 Copyright Act. Most of a library's needs to reproduce materials either for the library itself or for users is covered under § 108 of the Act. There are several matters that librarians want to clarify as they apply to digital works or to extend § 108's provisions to electronic works. For example, librarians want to use technological means to preserve copyrighted works. They want to be able to make electronic copies of works for users upon request just as they currently can produce photocopies of works under certain conditions. Librarians also want to be able to supply interlibrary loan copies electronically under the same conditions as they can provide photocopies today. They want to insure that users can browse digital works before any obligation to pay a fee for that use is triggered. And, jointly with faculty members, they want to be able to digitize current reserve collections to serve users better and to reduce the time, effort and storage space required by collections of reserve photocopies.

To this end, library associations have developed a joint statement on fair use in the electronic age which calls for recognition that the types of uses noted above are fair use.[20]

Preservation

Section 108 of the Copyright Act gives libraries that meet the § 108(a) requirements[21] the right to make copies of copyrighted works for preservation purposes in two instances. Under § 108(b), libraries may reproduce unpublished works for preservation, security or deposit for research in another library. Section 108(c), the replacement section, permits libraries to reproduce a published lost, damaged, stolen or deteriorating work after first making a reasonable effort to obtain an unused copy at a fair price. Both of these subsections indicate that the reproduction must be "in facsimile form." A photocopy of printed textual work certainly is a facsimile as is a microform copy. Both of these technologies are old, however, and libraries want to be able to use digital means to preserve library materials under conditions similar to those specified in subsections (b) and (c).

Is an electronic copy a facsimile? It can be argued that a scanned page which continues to look exactly like the printed page on the screen and from which a replica of the page can be printed is a facsimile. The difference, of course, is that the digital image can be used to reproduce printed copies, each of which will virtually be an original. Should libraries be restricted to the use of dated technology to preserve works held by the library? The materials which are sought to be preserved are no longer available from the publisher, and the library has already searched for an unused copy at a fair price.[22] One strategy librarians might adopt for obtaining the rights to use electronic means to preserve works is to seek acceptance of the proposition that scanned images are facsimiles.

Even without recognizing that digitized images are a facsimile copy, it still might be possible to reach agreements with the publishing community to permit digitization for preservation purposes. Some publishers have suggested that they would agree libraries should be able to reproduce works for preservation purposes under these conditions. They would, however, restrict the use of that digitized copy and require that the work cannot be accessed by users. To librarians this is ridiculous since the only reason to preserve a work is to ensure that users continue to be able to use it. Otherwise, there is little incentive to preserve the work. Librarians have proposed that any use of the digitized preservation copy be under the same conditions as the original work. In other words, users would have the same access and rights to use the work as they did before the work was preserved through digitization. Librarians might be willing to restrict use of those works to the institution and not permit interlibrary loan of the entire scanned work. Although the library could have loaned the original work, this restriction might satisfy publishers' concern about the creation of multiple copies from the scanned image. However, libraries should be able to loan through interlibrary loan an article from a journal, a chapter from a book or other small portion of the digitized work.

Electronic Copies for Users and Interlibrary Loan

Sections 108(d)-(e) permit libraries to reproduce copies of copyrighted works for users under certain conditions. For example, if the user requests no more than one article from a periodical issue or other collective work, the library may make a photocopy for the user. The copy must become the property of the user; the library must have no notice that the reproduction will be used for other than fair use purposes, and the library must display a warning sign containing the Register of Copyright's warning.[23] The library may even reproduce an entire work or a substantial portion thereof if the same three requirements listed above also are met. There is an additional requirement, however. The library must first determine by reasonable investigation that a copy cannot be obtained at a fair price.[24]

Clearly, the Copyright Act of 1976 was written before electronic copying was technologically possible. The Act, however, is technology neutral, and Congress tried very hard to ensure this neutrality.[25] The Act never uses the word "photocopy"; instead it uses the words "reproduce" or "copy." The word "photocopy" seldom appears even in the legislative history either. When it does it is only because that was the technology which existed at the time. The Register of Copyright's warning even says "libraries are authorized to furnish a photocopy or other reproduction"[26] which certainly indicates that the Register contemplated that copies might take the form of photocopies or other forms such as electronic copies. Why should libraries not be permitted to scan works and provide electronic copies to users upon request just as they can provide photocopies? There appears to be no reason either under the statute or in the legislative history why electronic copies should be prohibited. Clearly, libraries cannot retain the scanned image for reuse without permission of the copyright holder; this would be contrary to the requirements of subsections (d)-(e) which require that reproductions made become the property of the user.

Publishers are opposed to extending the provisions of § 108 to electronic copying by libraries because they fear that users who obtain an electronic copy will further transmit the copy to countless others. Is this any more likely than it is that users will further reproduce copies and distribute them? Maybe yes, maybe no. Users who follow the copyright law will not mass distribute electronic copies, and perhaps libraries could even help by including some statement along with the digitized copy to the effect that "no further distribution of the material is permitted."

Likewise, libraries are allowed under § 108(g)(2) and the Interlibrary Loan Guidelines[27] to borrow reproductions of copyrighted works from other libraries within the guideline's suggestion of five. Within a calendar year, the guidelines permit a library to borrow reproductions of five items from a periodical title going back five years.[28] If the lending library will not loan the original work, should it be limited to providing photocopies to satisfy the request? Why could an electronic copy not be sent? Libraries likely would support a requirement that the borrowing library must make a printed copy for the user and destroy the electronic copy just as the lending library is required to do under § 108(d).

Limiting the rights given to libraries by the technology is contrary to the purpose of the Act and to the desire of Congress to make the statute technologically neutral. Further, it seems more reasonable to find ways to permit this type of reproduction by including limiting statements about further distribution than to assume the copying should be prohibited.

Browsing

Currently the users of a library collection can browse through printed works and thus determine whether the work contains needed material. The user can simply read the work and extract needed information or reproduce the portions of the work needed for later use. As publishers make works available digitally and establish licensing arrangements to charge users for access to their works, librarians want to insure that the ability to browse works be continued in the electronic environment.

Publishers may choose to structure license agreements so that no user is permitted to access the work at all without triggering a fee. Librarians believe that research will be hampered if a user has to pay a fee in order to obtain access to the work even to determine if that work contains information which might be useful to the researcher. If a library subscribes to a work available only in digital format and agrees to pay for each use, should not there be some browsing of the work permitted before the fee must be paid? Librarians have suggested that users be charged for reproducing any portion of the work whether through downloading or printing but that the user be allowed to search the index and perhaps even to view abstracts before triggering the charge.

Not only will it benefit researchers to ensure that the ability to browse is preserved, but publishers also will benefit. If users are not permitted to view the index or a small portion of the work, researchers are likely to forego using the work at all. Thus, the publisher will receive no fees.

Electronic Reserve Collections

For years libraries have made photocopies of articles at the request of faculty members and placed them on reserve in the library to supplement the classroom as fair use. In 1982 the American Library Association produced the Reserve Guidelines at the request of libraries.[29] The guidelines are less authoritative than the other guidelines which have at least some stamp of Congress. On the other hand, the Reserve Guidelines have never been litigated which may mean there has been at least some tacit acceptance from the copyright holder community. The guidelines indicate that portions of copyrighted works can be reproduced for reserve even in multiple copies under conditions similar to those found in the Classroom Guidelines,[30] including that the same item is not placed on reserve in subsequent terms without permission from the copyright owner. In general the library should own a copy of the work it is reproducing for reserve collections. The Reserve Guidelines also specify that the number of copies should be reasonable in relation to the amount of other materials assigned for the course.[31] This important limitation clearly indicates that *all* of the material for a course should not be placed on reserve. It is not reasonable in relation to the other material assigned for the course. Thus, coursepacks or their equivalents should not be on reserve in lieu of having students purchase a textbook, purchase a coursepack or other materials for which the copyright owner receives royalties.

Another restriction is that the number of copies should be reasonable in relation to the number of students in the class, how quickly the material must be read and how much other material has been assigned to the class. This is further limited by the requirement from the general Classroom Guidelines that no more than one copy per student may be distributed. All reproductions for reserve must contain the notice of copyright. Further, the copying for reserve should not be detrimental to the market for the work.[32]

Many libraries have initiated electronic reserve collections in an effort to reduce the paperwork associated with maintaining photocopies, to enhance the accessibility of the collection and to facilitate students' learning. Libraries scan the works they normally would photocopy and create a database which may be searched by the student. Some schools limit use of the database to a few terminals in the library while others make the collection available over the campus network. Some libraries permit students either to download or to print a work from the database while some permit only printing. If the Reserve Guidelines are strictly followed, why should electronic reserve collections be a problem? Publishers' fears focus primarily on the potential for a student to transmit many thousands of copies of the work with a few key strokes. While this certainly is possible, it is unlikely. Perhaps there are steps libraries could take to allay these fears somewhat.

For example, if the database is to be made available over the campus network, the library could restrict access to only those students registered for the course. This could be done by issuing students an access code or using their student numbers to verify their registration for the course. A library can also restrict access by making the collection bibliographically unattractive. Instead of cataloging the item with a full bibliographic record that can be retrieved by author, title and subject, items could be listed only under the name of the faculty member and/or under the name and number of the course. Students should also be warned that materials retrieved from the electronic reserve collection are to be used only for educational purposes and that the student cannot further distribute or transmit the materials.

Going beyond the guidelines, such as repeating the item the second term, putting more material on reserve than is reasonable, etc., means that the faculty member must obtain permission from the copyright holder to retain the material for reuse in the electronic reserve collection. As faculty members want to move beyond reserve collections into electronic coursepacks, then it is no longer appropriate for the library to manage the collections as a reserve collection. Permission should be obtained and royalties paid for electronic coursepacks. It may prove more desirable for the university bookstore to manage the electronic coursepack, the charging of students for any royalties due and the forwarding of the royalties to the Copyright Clearance Center or directly to the copyright holder.

CONCLUSION

The library and education community continue to work to insure that students, faculty and library users have access to electronic works under conditions that approximate those specified for libraries and nonprofit educational institutions in the Copyright Act. Certainly there are differences in printed works and those that will be available only in digital form. These differences, however, are not so extreme that access and use of these works should be unduly restricted.

It is essential that both copyright holders and representatives of library and educational associations continue to talk with one another about how to accomplish the goals discussed in this article. Some of this has begun to occur through the fair use conferences suggested in the Green Paper by Bruce A. Lehman, U.S. Commissioner of Patent and Trademarks. The Green Paper called for education and library users of copyrighted works to work with the creator community much as occurred under the 1976 Act when the Classroom Guidelines were developed. Since October, 1994, representatives of various copyright holder groups have been meeting with representatives of library and education organizations to discuss whether it is possible to develop voluntary guidelines for fair use of electronic works. Although some progress has been made, it is too early to determine whether the conferences will be successful in the development of guidelines.

The instability of the technological age is one difficulty for the fair use conferences. Technology is changing so rapidly that it is almost impossible to develop very specific guidelines that will be applicable in a few years. Perhaps the solution will be general guidelines with agreement to re-visit them within three to five years. Most of the participants in these conferences remain hopeful that the conferences will be successful in reaching voluntary agreements between the user and the creator community.

NOTES

1. 17 U.S.C. §§ 1-1010 (1988).

2. *Intellectual Property and the National Information Infrastructure: A Preliminary Draft of the Report of the Working Group on Intellectual Property Rights* 9 (1994) [hereinafter Green Paper].

3. The eight categories of works are literary works; musical works; dramatic works; pantomimes and choreographic works; pictorial, graphic and sculptural works; motion pictures and other audiovisual works; sound recordings; and architectural works. 17 U.S.C. § 102(a) (1988).

4. *See Feist Publications v. Rural Telephone Services Co.*, 499 U.S. 340 (1991).

5. 17 U.S.C. § 102(a) (1988).

6. See *National Commission on New Technological Uses of New Copyrighted Works, Final Report* 44-46 (1979).

7. 17 U.S.C. § 106 (1988).

8. H.R. Rep. No. 1733, 94th Cong., 2d Sess. (1976) *reprinted in* 17 *Omnibus Copyright Revision Legislative History* 72-74 (1977) [hereinafter Conference Report].

9. 17 U.S.C. § 107 (1988).

10. H.R. Rep. No. 1476, 94th Cong., 2d Sess. (1976) *reprinted in* 17 *Omnibus Copyright Revision Legislative History* 68-70 (1977) [hereinafter House Report].

11. 758 F. Supp. 1522 (S.D.N.Y. 1991).

12. *Id.* at 1535-36.

13. Green Paper, *supra* note 2, at 60.

14. 17 U.S.C. § 110(1) (1988).

15. *Id.*

16. COREL advertises 200 CD-ROM's that contain 20,000 high resolution royalty-cleared photographs which are available for purchase for $699.00.

17. Because of the length of time it takes to create these works, a one-year use period without having to seek permission probably is not adequate.

18. *See* 17 U.S.C. § 110(2) (1988).

19. *Id.* § 102(a)(5).

20. *See Fair Use in the Electronic Age: Serving the Public Interest* in ARL: A Bimonthly Newsletter of Research Library Issues and Actions, March, 1995, at 5.

21. Libraries and archives must meet three requirements in order to qualify for the § 108 exemptions which permits making a single copy of a copyrighted work under certain circumstances: (1) The reproduction and distribution must not be for commercial advantage, either direct or indirect. (2) The collection must either be open to the public or to researchers doing research in the same field. (3) The reproduction and distribution must include notice of copyright. *See* 17 U.S.C. § 108(a) (1988).

22. 17 U.S.C. § 108(c) (1988).

23. *Id.* § 108(d). The Register's Warning may be found at 37 C.F.R. § 201.14 (1994).

24. *Id.* § 108(e). It should be noted that this section does not use the words "unused copy," so presumably the library would have to conduct a reasonable investigation of the used book market also for this work.

25. House Report, *supra* note 10, at 51.

26. 37 C.F.R. § 201.14 (1994).

27. Conference Report, *supra* note 8.

28. *Id.*

29. American Library Association, *Model Policy Concerning College and University Photocopying for Classroom, Research and Library Reserve Use* (1982) [hereinafter Reserve Guidelines], *reprinted in* 4 Coll. & Res. Lib. News 127-31 (1982).

30. House Report, *supra* note 10.

31. Reserve Guidelines, *supra* note 29.

32. *Id.*

Reporters' Rights and the Issue of Fair Use: The Rotbart Case

Anne F. Jennings

A recent decision by U.S. District Judge John S. Martin, Jr. in the Southern District of New York dismissed a copyright infringement and defamation case initiated by a former *Wall Street Journal* reporter against a public relations journal publisher. Although the opinion was not published, the Executive Director of the Reporters Committee for Freedom of the Press, Jane Kirtley, an attorney, stated that the decision "underscored the right of journalists to accurately report on speeches, writings and presentations that are of public interest and concern." Kirtley further allowed that the ruling "has taken a powerful tool of censorship from those who prefer not to have their presentations be subjected to public scrutiny."[1]

In *Dean Rotbart and TJFR Publishing Co., Inc. v. J. R. O'Dwyer Co., Inc. and Jack O'Dwyer,* 1995 WL 46625 (S.D.N.Y.), the plaintiff, Dean Rotbart alleges that articles published by the defendant Jack O'Dwyer in two of the defendant's publications infringed upon plaintiffs' copyright and defamed Mr. Rotbart. The defendants moved for summary judgment and on February 7, 1995, the motion was granted.

Dean Rotbart is President of the TJFR Publishing Co., Inc. which publishes a newsletter regarding journalism and offers seminars to professionals in the public relations industry. In particular, Rotbart offers a

---

Anne F. Jennings is a law librarian with the firm of Sinkler & Boyd in Charleston, South Carolina. She serves as Assistant to the Editor of *Against the Grain*, and is editor of a column on current issues in copyright litigation.

[Haworth co-indexing entry note]: "Reporters' Rights and the Issue of Fair Use: The Rotbart Case." Jennings, Anne F. Co-published simultaneously in *The Acquisitions Librarian* (The Haworth Press, Inc.) No. 15, 1996, pp. 89-93; and: *Current Legal Issues in Publishing* (ed: A. Bruce Strauch) The Haworth Press, Inc., 1996, pp. 89-93. Single or multiple copies of this article are available from The Haworth Document Delivery Service [1-800-342-9678, 9:00 a.m. - 5:00 p.m. (EST)].

workshop for executives called "Newsroom Confidential," for which all participants pay $350 each to attend. All public relation professionals who are present must sign a non-disclosure agreement before hearing Rotbart "advise on press relations and excoriate the financial press" for self-promotion and selling out to their sources. One of Rotbart's publications addresses financial journalism.[2]

O'Dwyer is the editor and publisher of *Jack O'Dwyer's Newsletter* and *O'Dwyer's PR Services Report.* Both the weekly newsletter and monthly report address news, people and other issues with regard to public relations matters.

On November 16, 1993, at the national conference of the Public Relations Society of America, Rotbart delivered an oral presentation which, although based in part on the typical "Newsroom Confidential" seminar, did not require the participants to sign a confidentiality agreement nor were there any other restrictions placed on the 200 plus registrants.

O'Dwyer attended the program and while there took handwritten notes and used a tape recorder as back-up. Subsequently, he wrote articles and editorials in three issues of the *Newsletter* and one issue of the *Report* addressing the events at the meeting. O'Dwyer both quoted and paraphrased Rotbart and was harshly critical of his ideas. Several members of the media later asked O'Dwyer for the context of Rotbart's quotations and O'Dwyer provided them with a transcript of the program which he had prepared from the audio-tape. A second version of the transcript was later sent out which corrected some of the errors contained in the first copy. It was undisputed that both versions were incomplete and contained some errors. Subsequent issues of the O'Dwyer publications reported reactions to the articles by media professionals. On February 18, 1994, following O'Dwyer's publication of all of the above-detailed articles, Rotbart registered his own transcription of the talk with the United States Copyright Office. On March 25, 1994, he filed suit against O'Dwyer.

This discussion will deal exclusively with the issue of copyright infringement/fair use, although it should be noted that summary judgment was granted as to the entire suit against the defendant, including allegations of unfair competition and defamation. Under 17 U.S.C. sec. 107, fair use is determined to be an equitable doctrine which allows reasonable use of copyrighted materials. The four statutory factors to be considered when determining fair use are: (1) purpose and character of the alleged use; (2) nature of the work; (3) extent of the copying; and (4) effect of the alleged infringement upon any potential market of the copyrighted work.

The Court's findings as to each of the four factors were as follows:

1. Purpose and character of the use: The preamble to section 107 of the U.S. Code specifically cites "criticism, comment, [and] news reporting" to be among the most appropriate purposes when determining a finding of fair use. The Court herein found that defendants used portions of Rotbart's presentation precisely for such purposes and further stated that "in the present case, the newsworthy and critical elements of Defendants' article outweigh" any commercial aspect. The primary reason Defendant wrote the articles was to provide a report on Rotbart's discussion and to express point of view commentary. Additionally, the Court found that O'Dwyer's works were not meant to supersede the use of the original work. Citing *Campbell v. Acuff-Rose Music, Inc.,* 114 S. Ct. 1164, 1171 (1994), O'Dwyer's fair use of the materials is further supported by the fact that his use added something new to plaintiffs' work, giving it a "different character . . . new expression, meaning or message." Acuff-Rose Music, holders of copyright to the song "Oh Pretty Woman," filed suit against Campbell and the rap music group 2 Live Crew claiming that the latter's song, "Pretty Woman," infringed the copyright of the original ballad written by the late Roy Orbison. The United States District Court for the Middle District of Tennessee and Judge Thomas A. Wiseman, Jr., initially granted the Defendant's Summary Judgment Motion and the copyright holders appealed. The case was subsequently reversed and remanded by the Court of Appeals, ruling that 2 Live Crew's parody of the original did not fit within the fair use doctrine requirements. Justice Souter, writing for the majority, stated that the "more transformative the new work, the less will be the significance of other factors, like commercialism, that may weigh against a finding of fair use" (1171).

Finally, with regard to this requirement, the Court found that it was not O'Dwyer's intention to make a profit by distributing the transcripts as they were initially recorded for his own use. By providing copies upon request, Defendants merely demonstrated that their reporting had been accurate. The limited distribution of the transcripts allowed readers to examine the published quotations in their own context and, therefore, to assume their own conclusions as to the authenticity of O'Dwyer's criticism.

2. Nature of the copyrighted work: This factor requires the court to consider whether a work is creative or factual, the fair use defense being narrower for more creative works. In the case at hand, the defendants contend that the talk by Rotbart was merely a factual guide. The Court disagreed, and found Rotbart's experience and ideas to be the primary source of this original work. However, the Court also found that the talk had been "de facto published," whereas the scope of fair use is narrower if a given work is unpublished. And, unlike previous presentations, Rotbart delivered the talk to a public forum of more than 200 people without requesting confidentiality. Also, Rotbart was aware of the presence of at least two reporters in the audience. In *Harper & Row Publishers, Inc. v. Nation Enterprises,* 471 U.S. 539, 105 S.Ct.2218 (1985), the Supreme Court held that in a given case, factors such as implied consent through de facto publication or performance or dissemination of a work may tip the balance of equities in favor of prepublication use. Therefore, as Rotbart had "published" his work at the proceeding, it was subject to fair use by the defendant.

The *Harper & Row* matter arose from an instance in which *The Nation* magazine received, from an unauthorized source, the unpublished manuscript of former President Gerald Ford's memoirs. *The Nation* thereafter published excerpts, in particular verbatim quotes, which detailed Ford's pardon of Richard Nixon. However, Harper & Row, the copyright holder of Mr. Ford's autobiography, had previously contracted with *Time* magazine to "pre-publish" certain excerpts, including those with regard to the pardon. The agreement between *Time* and Harper & Row included a $25,000 payment consisting of two installments, a $12,500 advance and $12,500 upon publication by *Time.* After *The Nation* intentionally "scooped" *Time*, the magazine withdrew its article and refused to pay Harper & Row the remaining $12,500. Thereafter, Harper & Row brought action against *The Nation* for copyright infringement and the U.S. District Court entered judgment in favor of the Plaintiffs. The Court of Appeals for the Second Circuit reversed and Harper & Row petitioned for Writ of Certiorari. In an opinion by Justice Sandra Day O'Connor, the Supreme Court reversed and remanded holding that the "magazine's unauthorized publication of verbatim quotes from essentially the 'heart' of unpublished presidential memoirs, which was intended to supplant copyright holders' commercially valuable right of first publication was not 'fair use'" (2218).

With regard to the second factor, Nature of the Copyrighted Work, Justice O'Connor stated that the scope of fair use is narrower with regard to unpublished works; in particular, an author has the right to control the first public appearance of his expression. Such is not the case in *Rotbart* wherein the Court found that the plaintiff had, in effect, "pre-published" his talk at the conference before the Public Relations Society.

3. Amount and substantiality of work used: This factor requires consideration of both quantitative and qualitative substantiality. Relevant is the amount and substantiality after an expression has been used and not the factual content. Rotbart's presentation was over 14,000 words and defendants published a total of 793 words with no single article quoting more than 602 words. Plaintiffs contended that O'Dwyer stole "the heart" of the presentation, but the Court allowed that this particular issue alone, if true, is not sufficient to satisfy the third fair use factor. This issue, as addressed by Justice Souter in *Campbell v. Acuff-Rose Music, Inc.* (1168), was given insufficient consideration with regard to the "nature of parody in weighing the *degree of copying*" (emphasis added) and was the primary cause for the Supreme Court's reversal and remand. Therein, the Court found that the amount of reasonable copying depended on, among others, how much the copy served "as a market substitute for the original" (1175). In the case at hand, the Court found it extremely doubtful that anyone would accept O'Dwyer's news report as a substitute.

4. Effect of the use on market value: The Supreme Court in *Stewart v. Abend,* 110 S.Ct. 1750, 1769 (1990) (quoting 3 *Nimmer on Copyright* sec. 13.05[A]) has determined this final factor to be "the most important, and indeed, central fair use factor." (*Stewart* primarily addressed the issue of assignment of rights when an author dies prior to the copyright renewal period. In such an instance, the Court held that regardless of the author's previous assignment, when one dies before the time for renewal, his statutory benefits become the holders of the renewal rights.) The defense of fair use is allowable in such cases as where the Defendants' use of Plaintiffs' work does not diminish its potential sales or fulfill the demand of the original work. In this case, Rotbart argued that the direct competition by the parties and the use by Defendant of information which disparaged Plaintiff is both Plaintiffs' loss and Defendants' gain. The Court, deferring to 3 *Nimmer on Copyright* sec. 13.05[A][4] (1994), held that it is not necessary for a court to "take into account an adverse impact on the potential market for Plaintiff's work by reason of disparaging or otherwise unfavorable reference in Defendant's work to Plaintiff's work . . . The fourth factor looks to adverse impact only by reason of usurpation of the demand for Plaintiff's work through Defendant's copying of protectible expression from such work." In *Rotbart,* Plaintiffs' argument as to the Defendants' campaign to damage his reputation is not relevant and once O'Dwyer's use is determined to be fair use, his purpose in doing so is unimportant.

While unpublished opinions do not hold the same weight as those which appear in the official reporters, this summary judgment decision, which supports the rights of the press and their ability to accurately report the news, is significant to the publishing industry and provides an excellent examination of the fair use doctrine as it applies to de facto publication, the purpose of the publication, and the amount of the work used. The facts presented here clearly support the Court's dismissal of Plaintiffs' claims and the rights of reporters.

NOTES

1. Garneau, George, "Court Upholds Newsletter in 'Fair Use' Case," *Editor & Publisher* 128 (Febuary 25, 1995): 22.
2. *Ibid.*

LICENSING

Legal Aspects of Electronic Publishing: Look Both Ways Before Crossing the Street

Glen M. Secor

INTRODUCTION

Protection of intellectual property rights begins not when a work is published and placed into the market, but rather when the work is being developed. This paper will address some of the critical legal issues facing publishers and others in the acquisition and development of content for electronic publishing, including multimedia publishing. Special attention will be paid to the interests of publishers and authors in the various transactions involved in developing digital works.

Beginning with traditional book contracts and continuing through electronic publishing development agreements and multimedia joint ventures, the author will examine the emerging rights issues in electronic publish-

Glen M. Secor is with Yankee Book Peddler, 999 Maple Street, Contoocook, NH 03229.

[Haworth co-indexing entry note]: "Legal Aspects of Electronic Publishing: Look Both Ways Before Crossing the Street." Secor, Glen M. Co-published simultaneously in *The Acquisitions Librarian* (The Haworth Press, Inc.) No. 15, 1996, pp. 95-110; and: *Current Legal Issues in Publishing* (ed: A. Bruce Strauch) The Haworth Press, Inc., 1996, pp. 95-110. Single or multiple copies of this article are available from The Haworth Document Delivery Service [1-800-342-9678, 9:00 a.m. - 5:00 p.m. (EST)].

ing. The focus throughout is on developing the business relationships and securing the rights needed to publish electronic works.

ELECTRONIC RIGHTS IN AUTHOR-PUBLISHER BOOK CONTRACTS

One approach to the acquisition of electronic publishing rights is to simply include them with the transfer of traditional print rights. Publishers have long sought to do this with the "all media now in existence or hereinafter discovered" clause of the typical book contract, meaning that the publisher acquired the rights to the book in print and electronic form. Ten or twenty years ago that clause may not have meant much to authors, or perhaps even to publishers. But with new media being developed on a near constant basis, and with electronic publishing seeming to be the wave of the future, electronic rights are no longer an afterthought in book contracts. Now publishers, authors, and agents are finding that electronic rights often do not fit neatly into the traditional book contract.

The National Writers Union has developed a "Statement of Principles on Contracts Between Writers and Electronic Book Publishers" (National Writers Union, 1993). This Statement is useful not only because of the specific positions being advanced by the NWU, some of which will be discussed here, but moreover for the list of issues which it addresses. These issues, using the NWU's section headings, are: 1. Copyright, 2. Grant of Rights, 3. Creative Control, 4. Manuscript Acceptance, 5. Royalties, 6. Royalty Statements, 7. Termination, 8. Option, 9. Non-competition, 10. Arbitration, and 11. Affordability and Access. This section will focus on certain of these topics, but the analysis is not limited to the issues specifically raised in the NWU proposal.

Copyright

Copyright is not an issue, per se, simply because a work is to be adapted to electronic form or because it is prepared originally in electronic form. Authors and other creators own the copyrights in the works which they create. They transfer the rights in their works, usually in return for remuneration, to publishers, movie studios, television studios, and others who are positioned to exploit those works. Electronic publishers, some of whom will also be print publishers, will be among the potential transferees of rights.

Copyright becomes more complex not because of the electronic publication of a work, but because of the potential for collaboration among creators and integration of various works which exist in the electronic environment. This is the whole essence of the "multimedia" movement. For electronic publishers, the new trick to copyright, if there is one, is in keeping track of who owns which rights in what elements of the electronic work. This task is obviously at its most complex in a true multimedia work combining various forms of content from a multitude of sources, but also must be managed for a pure text work for which there are multiple contributors or to which is added proprietary search software.

The NWU position on copyright in electronic publishing agreements is that the author should control copyright, as he does in the print environment, until he or she makes a complete or partial transfer of such rights. The NWU proposal acknowledges "work-for-hire" situations as exceptions to this norm. As will be discussed in the sections below, work-for-hire and other types of author-publisher arrangements may become more prevalent in the electronic world.

MORAL RIGHTS

The issue of "moral rights" is looming larger in the U.S. copyright picture and poses particular problems in the electronic environment. Moral rights are essentially authors' rights in the paternity and integrity of their works. Moral rights are given more weight in other copyright regimes, particularly those of European countries, but the international nature of trade in intellectual property and the U.S. accession to the Berne Convention have increased their importance here. While U.S. law generally does not provide for explicit moral rights, the Visual Artists Rights Act, 17 U.S.C. 106A, does provide such rights for works of fine art (Greguras et al., 1994).

There is an undeniable tension between the legal trend toward moral rights and the practical reality of new information technologies. Because of the ease with which electronic information can be manipulated and passed along, it would seem more difficult for publishers to safeguard the moral rights of authors in the electronic world than in the print environment. Anyone who participates in online discussion groups or newsgroups has doubtlessly witnessed instances of manipulation or improper attribution of quotes.

As will be discussed below, in the section on clearing rights, publishers must be careful how they use copyrighted works in their electronic publications. What the publisher considers to be necessary and appropriate editing, perhaps by using only a portion of a film clip, still photo, or sound clip, might be unacceptable to the author or performer. This could be a problem even if licensor of the material to the publisher, say the movie studio or the art house, regards the use as acceptable. Remember that moral rights are author rights and do not travel with the copyright. The examples presented here might not pose a legal problem for the publisher in the U.S., but could elsewhere in the world.

The issue of moral rights must also be considered in the distribution of electronic works. Publishers need to be aware of their obligations to protect moral rights and must take reasonable steps to meet those obligations. What constitutes reasonable protection remains to be determined, but the possibilities range from the relatively simple to the extremely burdensome. When the publisher licenses a work for end use, or sublicenses it for inclusion in another publisher's work, it might be sufficient to include a statement of moral rights in the license, thereby placing the burden of protecting those rights on the licensee. When a publisher distributes material online, it might be necessary to encrypt the material to ensure authenticity. These matters need to be resolved as the law and the technology continue to develop in the coming years.

Granting and Termination of Rights

The granting and termination of electronic rights is clearly one of the biggest sources of potential conflict between publishers and authors in book contracts. As indicated above, the "all media now in existence or hereinafter discovered" clause does not fly anymore. Few authors are willing to give up such sweeping rights, especially to print publishers whose ability to produce and market electronic works is unproven at best. The difference between print rights and electronic rights is profound in this area.

When we talk about print rights to a book, even a trade book with significant commercial appeal, we are really talking variations on a single theme. Paperback rights, mass market rights, foreign rights, serial rights, reprint rights, etc., all involve the same fundamental product–a print book. The formats, for the most part, are long-established and do not change much. Movie rights and other dramatic rights in the story are generally handled separate of the print rights.

"Electronic print rights," though, are different. Electronic formats are evolving and will continue to do so. Publishers, whose ability to exploit the electronic formats of today is largely unproven, may or may not keep pace with the developments in technology. The publisher who develops a successful CD-ROM publishing program today may miss the boat on online publishing tomorrow. It is quite understandable that authors are reluctant to enter into long-term transfers of electronic rights in the midst of such uncertainty.

Electronic rights also differ from print in that one of the great terminating events of the print contract, "out of print" status, perhaps ceases to be in the electronic world. When a print book is "out of stock" and no further printings are planned, the book is clearly out of print. It is difficult to classify as in print or out of print a book which exists in digital form and is accessible electronically.

In this context, the NWU proposals on the granting and termination of electronic rights seem to make sense. First, electronic rights should terminate if they are not exploited within a reasonable and stated period of time by the publisher. A publisher who does not develop an electronic publishing program, or who does not include a particular work within such a program, should not be allowed to sit on the electronic rights to that work (see also Curtis, 1991). Further, because publishers may not keep pace with the changes in technology, electronic rights should be granted for much shorter periods of time than the duration of the print rights. Finally, "out of print" status should be replaced by "out of promotion" status, meaning that the publisher is no longer marketing the work and rights should revert to the author.

The provisions, of course, may not seem quite so sensible to the publisher. In the electronic arena, the publisher is dealing essentially with the same uncertainties as the author. No one really knows how the technology and markets will develop. The economics of electronic publishing are very dicey, with many pointing to big potential profits down the road, but few (if any) earning them today. Publishers run huge risks of investing too much or too little in their electronic publishing programs.

Publishers also run risks in not acquiring electronic rights or in acquiring those rights for short durations. Take, for example, a professional book, science book, or textbook with significant backlist or revised edition potential. Assume that the title is expected to sell for ten years or longer. Assume further that no significant market exists for the title in electronic form today.

Can anyone look even a decade into the future and be certain that no electronic market will develop for the title during that time? Probably not. But what if, because of all the concerns outlined above, the author is willing to grant the electronic rights for only five years? The publishing house could find itself in a position of losing the electronic rights around the time that the electronic market for the title develops. The publisher, after largely making the market for the title through sales of the print edition during the first five years of publication, could see the print edition facing competition down the road from someone else's electronic edition. And the publisher could lose the electronic rights even if it was reasonably positioned to exploit them, because of, say, an unrelated dispute with the author, or because the author honestly believes another company is better suited to bring out the electronic edition.

No, the segregation of print and electronic rights is not as simple or "fair" as it might first appear. And if we project far enough into the future, when a book might be available in any number of different formats and via many means (e.g., printed and bound, printed on demand, online, on CD-ROM or other storage media, etc.), it is hard to imagine a publisher making the primary editorial and marketing commitment to the book without having all or most of these rights during the return on investment period.

So, we find ourselves in an age of uncertainty over who should control the electronic rights to texts. Uncertainty breeds risk, and the essence of this dilemma is allocating the risks between publishers and authors. Various author and publisher groups have argued that one side or the other should always control electronic print rights, but it is doubtful that any such absolute approach can succeed. These matters, at least for the time being, seem destined to be negotiated on a case by case basis. The nature and electronic publishing potential of the work, the potential market for the work, and the expertise and track record of the publisher are some of the factors which must be taken into consideration in deciding who should get which electronic rights and for how long.

SUBLICENSES AND TRANSFERS

Of course, a publishing house, even if it holds the electronic publishing rights to various works, may not develop the capability to effectively exploit all of those rights. The markets for electronic books are just developing and few, if any, publishers will be able to establish themselves in all potential markets in the foreseeable future. Therefore, we will likely see a healthy market for sublicensing and transfer of these rights. Such a trend, though, could fly in the face of author desires, as indicated in the NWU proposal, to keep a tight leash on these rights and creative control over the electronic projects in which their works are used. Sublicensing or transfer by the primary publisher of the rights of all or part of a work may represent the author's best chance at having the work successfully exploited in the electronic marketplace. Still, authors may be reluctant to give publishers the unfettered right to enter into such sublicenses and transfers.

One approach to this problem would be to make transfers and sublicenses of the electronic rights subject to the approval of the author, which could not be unreasonably withheld. Some print book contracts contain such a provision regarding the primary publishing rights. Publishers, however, might find this requirement to be burdensome, especially if the volume of permissions and sublicensing is great. In that event, publisher rights and permissions departments will probably be struggling to keep up with the volume of requests, never mind having to clear each transaction with the author.

The International Publishers Copyright Council, in the report from its Third International Copyright Symposium (held in May 1994, in Turin), suggests a hierarchy of electronic rights which authors and publishers should agree upon. This hierarchy would consist of "prime rights" and "subsidiary rights" (International Publishers Copyright Council, 1994). Prime rights would be the right "to issue a copyright work on electronic media" (i.e., the right of the publisher to publish in electronic form) and the right "to authorize the storage of a copyright work in any medium by electronic means" (e.g., to allow a document delivery service to store a digital copy of the work for printing and delivery to its customers). Subsidiary rights would include the right of the publisher to include the work in "another publisher's/producer's electronic product or service" or in "multimedia works," and to authorize the downloading, distribution, or networking of the work by third parties, as well as certain other rights.

Publishers and authors could utilize this hierarchy of rights to determine which rights can be sublicensed or transferred by the publisher with or without the author's permission. The prime right "to issue a copyright work on electronic media," for instance, might never be transferable without the author's approval. The right of the publisher to license the work or a portion thereof for inclusion in another publisher's electronic product or in a multimedia work might require the author's assent in some instances but not in others. By recognizing the various prime and subsidiary rights, and by negotiating up-front any limitations on the publisher's ability to sublicense or transfer those rights, publishers and authors will avoid unnecessary surprises or disputes over the use of the published work.

Royalties

Of course, if the economics can be made to work to everyone's advantage, then concerns over the granting of electronic rights would diminish. Unfortunately, that situation does not exist today. If the early positions on royalties are any indication, economics may be the most contentious aspect of electronic publishing.

The NWU position on royalties is predictable and somewhat understandable: royalty rates on electronic books should be higher than on print books, to reflect the lower production costs on electronic books. Royalty rates on books sold online should be even higher, to reflect the lower costs of network distribution. After all, it is clearly cheaper to produce a copy of a CD-ROM disk than to produce a copy of a print book, or to transmit a book electronically versus shipping a print book.

The problem with this position is that it takes such a narrow view of production and distribution costs. Even if we assume for the moment that editorial and marketing costs are similar for electronic books and print books, and that the actual physical production and distribution of copies is cheaper in the electronic world, it still does not follow that electronic books cost less to publish than print books. There are development costs associated with electronic books, including software and other technical development costs, which may not be present in print books. Even in the case of online distribution, there are tremendous costs associated with data storage and transmission. These costs cannot be overlooked in the demand for higher author royalties.

The NWU also advocates the payment of royalties based upon the list price of the electronic book, rather than on the net price, as is the case for print books. One exception to royalties-on-list would be for the sale of copies which are bundled by hardware manufacturers for sale with the machines themselves. The rationale given for royalties-on-list is that royalties-on-net allows too much potential for publisher abuse and creates suspicions in the minds of authors.

There is a reason for the current royalties-on-net approach, of course. The book distribution and selling process in this country has utilized discount-off-list pricing, including now at the retail level. The list price persists, despite the fact that no one in the buying chain, except sometimes the individual consumer, pays it anymore.

If books, like most other consumer goods, came without a "manufacturer's list price," we would not be having this debate over the appropriate base for author royalties. But semantics aside, it is hard to understand why author royalties would be based on anything other than publisher revenues from the sale of the books. Publishers, one assumes, are in the business of maximizing their revenues per title. Discounts are given, presumably, to increase the volume of books in the distribution chain and to maximize dollar sales. Author royalties are maximized when publisher sales are maximized. Publisher sales, like sales for every other manufacturer, distributor, retailer, or service company, are booked at net.

As unsatisfying as the NWU position on royalties on electronic books might be, it is no more so than that reportedly adopted by Harcourt Brace for the electronic versions of some of its print books. A dispute between Harcourt and one of its authors, NWU member Larry Bailey, has resulted in a lawsuit. Harcourt is asserting that it is not obligated to pay royalties on the digital versions of two accounting books which Bailey wrote or co-wrote, as Bailey's contract specifies royalties only for print editions (Reid, 1994). Harcourt took this position after Bailey had rejected Harcourt's offer for a substantially reduced royalty for the digital edition.

What is most interesting about this dispute is Harcourt's rationale for pushing the reduced royalty in the first place. According to a Harcourt spokesperson, the reduced royalty is needed because "electronic versions have significant development costs and the software firms that designed them are assigned a royalty as payment" (Reid, 1994).

Yes, but what about the lower production and distribution costs which the NWU cites as justification for higher author royalties on electronic books?

Electronic publishing is a relatively new game and its economics are unclear. One cannot help but sense a bit of opportunism by publishers and authors in the face of this lack of clarity. Each side is pointing to the elements of the cost equation which support its argument for higher or lower author royalties. Neither side seems to be acknowledging the entire cost equation, however uncertain it might be.

What is needed here, rather than opportunism, is realism and an open sharing of information. The electronic rights clauses of many, many existing book contracts are ticking time bombs. The importance of electronic rights and royalties in book contract negotiations will only increase in the future. If either side goes too far in trying to exploit the situation, in individual transactions or in the aggregate, author-publisher relations will suffer immeasurably. The evidence thus far indicates that both sides may be headed in that unfortunate direction.

THE ART OF THE MULTIMEDIA DEAL

Electronic publishing forces us to think not only about the terms of the traditional book contract, but also about the very nature of the author-publisher relationship and the role of each in the process. In the print world, most author-publisher transactions involve the arms-length transfer of rights and money, although a different relationship, usually under a work-for-hire arrangement, is possible. In the electronic environment, publishers will find themselves entering into many more transactions which do not involve the outright acquisition of intellectual property. Some of these will consist of the licensing of content for specific and limited purposes, which is a presentation unto itself and will not be dealt with here.

Development Agreements

Other transactions will actually increase the publishers' control over the content of its digital publications. These arrangements, essentially a variation of work-for-hire, are accomplished via development agreements. Print publishers who want to become successful electronic publishers will have to become familiar with the use of development agreements.

The role of the author into the digital and multimedia world is the source of much speculation and debate within the publishing industry. Some experts have predicted that authorship will change from a process of linear story telling (or explanation of facts) to one of multimedia integration, with the "text" serving primarily to navigate the "reader" through new multimedia worlds (Curtis, 1991). Under this view, the author of text will function not as an independent creator of content, but as part of a development and production team, with others contributing graphics, sound, interactivity, etc. The product produced by this team could be influenced equally by any of the team members; the "story" would not necessarily control. One could argue that such an approach to authorship already exists in movies and television, with very spotty results.

This change in the nature of authorship may or may not occur on a broad scale, but it is already happening in subtle ways even in today's relatively simple digital text publishing projects. For example, in the Harcourt Brace-Bailey dispute mentioned above, the author is apparently doing annual updates on the books under a work-for-hire contract. As also mentioned above, Harcourt is pushing for lower author royalties because it must also pay royalties to the software firms involved in the project.

This type of arrangement, which is essentially an ongoing development and production team for these electronic books, will become more common as the volume of digital text publishing grows. The media in this case is the floppy disk. CD-ROM versions of the book would likely bring more and different players to the team, as would online publication.

In the context of author-publisher agreements, we must keep in mind that electronic publishing involves more than simply "printing" the text in another format. Digitization of a text does not alter its fundamental characteristics, but adding hypertext links does. Adding graphics and sound changes the nature of the work even further. When the objective of a project is not to simply digitize an existing textbook, for instance, but rather to develop an interactive CD-ROM for the teaching of a subject, one dimension of which might be the material contained in that textbook, then the role of the text and its author have changed fundamentally.

Development agreements are one means by which a publisher can specify and coordinate the roles of the various parties involved in an electronic publishing project. They can be used to control the work of in-house personnel, under work-for-hire arrangements, as well as of independent suppliers. Software publishers have long used them for software development projects, which tend to involve both in-house development, outsourcing, and third-party licensing. Electronic publishing projects in this sense can be managed similarly to software development projects.

An in-depth discussion of development agreements and the many provisions which can be included in them is beyond the scope of this paper. For a solid explanation of such agreements, including a good sample agreement, I recommend the handbook *Multimedia: Law and Practice* by Michael D. Scott (Prentice-Hall Law and Business, 1993). In fact, I will use the format of Mr. Scott's analysis in the following overview.

Successful electronic publishing development agreements begin with effective functional and detailed specifications of the product. The specifications, which can be used internally and with any outside party participating in the project, must clearly state not only what the product is to do, what it is to look like, and how it is to work, but also how the development project itself is to be accomplished.

Product specifications might include a general description of the title, the media and operating system(s) on which the title will run, the number and types of graphics expected to be incorporated, the expected search and linking capabilities, the volume of text to be included, expected printing and downloading capabilities, rough screen layouts, compatibility with word processors and other types of software, networkability, packaging, after-sale customer support et al. Project specifications would address such issues as file formats, security, documentation, testing, training, deadlines, budgets, confidentiality (i.e., re: product information and trade secrets learned during development), change procedures, etc.

Many of these specifications would be incorporated, directly or via addendum, in the development agreement. Their utility is less legal than practical, though. Whatever the nature of the electronic publishing project, whether it is a simple text on floppy disk or a full-blown multimedia CD-ROM, and no matter what combination of in-house and outside resources are being used, the specifications serve as the map for the project, indicating both the destination and the route which is to be taken. It is, of course, essential that any changes made to the specifications over the course of the project be communicated to all participants promptly.

The development contract or contracts must clearly delineate responsibility for all aspects of the project and for ongoing maintenance of the product. Who is responsible for writing the captions for any still photos which are used in the title? Who is responsible for updating the text and graphics? Who is responsible for customer technical support? Who is responsible for making/obtaining all necessary licenses and clearances for copyrighted material being used in the work? What happens if the search software ceases to run or run effectively on future generations of operating systems? Even in the simplest of electronic publishing projects, the publisher, author, and software supplier(s) must know who is responsible for what.

Beyond specifying the product and allocating the various project responsibilities, the biggest issue facing the parties to an electronic book development agreement is sorting out who will own what aspects of the final product. Ownership of any content which is licensed for use in the product will be clear and will be governed by the licenses. Ownership of content or functional software which is developed specifically for the product may be less clear. Does the author of the text own the text which she writes for inclusion in the electronic book, or was she brought in on a work-for-hire basis, with all rights to the text being owned by the publisher? If the text includes forms, say accounting forms, who owns the software which the outside software firm develops to allow end users to fill out forms online?

There are legal tests and standards which a court can apply to the specific facts and circumstances of a case to settle disputes over ownership. The parties to the development agreement should avoid such disputes altogether by agreeing from the outset who will own the various components of the final product.

Ownership issues are critical to pricing, as well as use. If the software firm is to own the forms software at the end of the project, and if it believes that it can sell that software to other publishers for use in their electronic accounting texts, then the firm is likely to charge less for developing the program than if it does not own the software. If the publisher does not want to have other publishers using the program, it will presumably be willing to pay more in development fees in order to secure ownership. But if the software firm is to own the software at the end of the project, the publisher should insist on some sort of license which allows it to use the program for a certain period of time without having to pay any additional licensing fee.

The parties are free to allocate ownership in the elements of the final product any way they choose. They should do so right from the outset in order to avoid misunderstandings and disputes.

My point in this section has not been to identify all of the issues which must or should be addressed in an electronic publishing development agreement. Rather, the intention has been to indicate the complexity of multi-party development projects, and to show how they differ from a simple two-party author-publisher book contract. On some electronic publishing projects, all transactions will occur at arms' length and issues of responsibility and ownership will be clear, i.e., when the publisher acquires the content from the author, licenses the software from the software firm, then handles the tasks of digitizing the text and integrating the software in-house. There, the legal agreements between the parties can be very straightforward. In other circumstances, as I have tried to indicate, the transactions, along with issues of responsibility and ownership, will be more complicated. The best response to this complexity is a clear and comprehensive development agreement.

Acquiring and Clearing Electronic Rights

Electronic publishing is essentially the marrying of content and software. Multimedia publishing expands the types of content significantly and the sources for that content exponentially. Because of the software component and the addition of non-text media to the content mix, intellectual property issues in electronic publishing are vastly more numerous and complex than in traditional print publishing. A full review and legal analysis of these issues is beyond the scope of this paper, but publishers should be aware of the following major points.

As has been discussed above, electronic publishing projects are likely to involve collaboration with software firms and developers, as well as with other providers of content. Some electronic publishing programs, as well as individual electronic publishing projects in other programs, will be structured as or at least will function similarly to joint ventures. Each party to the venture must realize the following: the rights of the venture in the content which it publishes will only be as good as the rights of the party which contributed that content. Further, if the work produced by the venture is found to infringe or violate the intellectual property rights of a third party, the venture and not merely the party which contributed the infringing material will be liable. This means that each participant in an electronic publishing venture must be confident not only in its own rights in the property which it contributes, but also in the rights of all of the participants in the property which each contributes.

When business enterprises agree to form a joint venture, the parties to the joint venture generally conduct some form of due diligence on each other. This might involve looking into the finances of the other joint venture partners, interviewing the various management teams involved, physically inspecting one another's assets, etc. When companies and individuals come together in an electronic publishing venture, whether it be an ongoing publishing program or just a single publishing project, they should be concerned about the financial health and other key characteristics of the partners, but should also conduct due diligence on the intellectual property being brought in to the venture.

In an excellent article entitled "Intellectual Property Due Diligence for Multimedia Strategic Alliances," William Tanenbaum explains not only why such due diligence is necessary, but also what it should seek to accomplish (Tanenbaum, 1994). Attorney Tanenbaum's 12-point checklist of subjects to be addressed in due diligence is so valuable that it is duplicated here:

1. Whether the venture party owns the contributed property, or has a license right sufficient to grant the alliance the right to exploit the property in the intended manner.
2. Whether the intellectual property rights in the contributed property are valid and enforceable.
3. Whether any third party has any intellectual property rights in the property, and if so, what the nature of the interest is.
4. Whether the contributing party is bound by any agreement, obligation or restriction which would prevent it from granting the intended rights in the property contributed to the venture.
5. Whether the contributing party (or other owner) has "perfected" the intellectual property rights through proper registrations, recordations, and other filings in the United States patent, copyright, and trademark offices, and if applicable, in offices of foreign governments.
6. Whether there are defects in any such filings which need to be corrected.
7. Whether intellectual property rights have been and are being properly kept in force through the timely payment of patent maintenance fees and the like, both in the United States and abroad.
8. Whether the venture's exploitation of the contributed property will infringe an intellectual property right of a third party.
9. Whether the contributed property is the subject of any past, pending, or threatened litigation, and if so, what the effect of this is, or is likely to be, on the venture's intended marketing of the contributed property.
10. Whether there are any aspects of the contributing party's past or current licensing practices which give rise to patent or copyright mis-

use or which would otherwise render the intellectual property rights in the contributed property unenforceable.
11. Whether the contributing party has obtained proper United States and foreign moral rights waivers, permissions to use actors' likenesses, and permissions from entertainment industry guilds, unions, and the like.
12. Whether the contributed property is subject to any existing or contingent security interests or similar encumbrances.

I strongly encourage the legal or rights department of every publisher to pick up a copy of the complete text of this article and to consider a subscription to *The Computer Lawyer*, which has included a number of excellent articles about multimedia rights in recent months.

Notice the breadth of intellectual property rights mentioned in the checklist, as well as the various aspects of these rights which should be investigated. The introduction of software to the equation raises the issue of patents, something with which most print publishers have probably not dealt. Inclusion of stills, film clips, and sound clips necessitates consideration of right to likeness, right of publicity, trademark, etc. Intellectual property protection in electronic publishing encompasses more than traditional copyright protection.

FACILITATING THE LICENSING, SUBLICENSING, AND END-USER LICENSING OF ELECTRONIC WORKS

Time and space do not allow for fuller consideration of this topic, but the following sources should be of interest to publishers and others involved in electronic publishing:

The Copyright Clearance Center (CCC) "Rightsholder Electronic Access Agreement," which establishes CCC as a possible clearinghouse for electronic subrights pursuant to the appropriate grant of rights to CCC from the publisher.

Mark L. Gordon and Timothy P. Walsh, "Transaction-Based Licenses: Managing Revenues and Controlling Costs," *The Computer Lawyer*, v. 11, no. 10 (Oct. 94).

Fred Greguras and Sandy J. Wong, "Software Licensing Complements the Digital Age," a paper made available by the Electronic Frontier Foundation (EFF) via the World Wide Web (http://www.eff.org) or by contacting EFF and requesting a copy.

"Negotiating Networked Information Contracts and Licenses," a draft paper prepared by Robert Ubell Associates for the Coalition for Networked Information (CNI) as part of CNI's READI program (Rights for Electronic Access to and Delivery of Information). This outstanding document, dated Nov. 15, 1994, examines a comprehensive set of terms and issues which should be addressed in any networked use license. Available from CNI via the WWW (http://www.cni.org) or by contacting CNI and requesting a copy.

SUMMARY

This paper has addressed a number of legal and business issues relating to the acquisition of intellectual property for the purpose of electronic publishing, at best scratching the surface of any of them. Electronic rights will be one of the most difficult issues publishers will face in the electronic world. A successful transition from the legal practices which have developed in the print world to those which will be required in the electronic world will depend upon the degree of openness and understanding which all involved, including authors, publishers, software firms, and others, bring to the table. Some of the issues involved with electronic publishing will resolve themselves easily, while others will require ongoing negotiation and careful balancing of a number of potentially competing interests. Awareness of the law and the underlying business realities will be essential to the development of a sensible legal framework for electronic publishing.

REFERENCES

Richard Curtis, "Here Come the Cyberbooks: Future of Publishing Glimpsed Through New Contract Clause," Locus, the Newspaper of the Science Fiction Field, 1991.

Fred Greguras, Michael R. Egger, and Sandy J. Wong, "Multimedia and the Superhighway: Rapid Acceleration or Foot on the Brake?," The Computer Lawyer, v. 11, no. 9 (Sept. 94).

International Publishers Copyright Council, "The Publisher in the Electronic World" (a report for The Third IPA International Copyright Symposium), 1994.

Calvin Reid, "NWU Calls Harcourt Unfair in Digital Royalty Dispute," Publishers Weekly, Dec. 12, 1994.

William A. Tanenbaum, "Intellectual Due Diligence for Multimedia Strategic Alliances," The Computer Lawyer, v. 11, no. 10 (Oct. 94).

Evaluating Existing and Implied Licenses for On-Line Distribution Rights

Charisse Castagnoli

INTRODUCTION

Copyright law has been a part of our country's jurisprudence since the Constitution was first enacted. The purpose of the copyright law is to provide monetary rewards for authors to bring their works to the public and thus support the marketplace of ideas necessary for a democratic society.[1] To further this policy, the Copyright statute grants five exclusive rights to authors: the right to distribute the work; the right to reproduce the work; the right to create derivative works; the right to perform the work publicly; and the right to display the work publicly.[2] The Copyright owner may also transfer, assign, or license all or part of these exclusive rights.[3] If the work is licensed, ownership is retained by the copyright owner while specific use rights are granted the licensee.

Since copyright licenses have the effect of apportioning economic rights, a tension between copyright owners and existing licensees unfolds whenever a new medium is created for those copyrighted works. In this context, copyright owners assert that no license has been granted for the new medium, while licensees counter that the new use was included or was intended to be included in the existing license grant. Exemplifying this conflict is the battle over television rights in the 1950s and 60s.

Charisse Castagnoli is an intellectual property attorney employed by Haystack Laboratories in Austin, Texas. She has worked in the computer industry in the areas of software development and marketing for a number of Unix-based systems.

[Haworth co-indexing entry note]: "Evaluating Existing and Implied Licenses for On-Line Distribution Rights." Castagnoli, Charisse. Co-published simultaneously in *The Acquisitions Librarian* (The Haworth Press, Inc.) No. 15, 1996, pp. 111-121; and: *Current Legal Issues in Publishing* (ed: A. Bruce Strauch) The Haworth Press, Inc., 1996, pp. 111-121. Single or multiple copies of this article are available from The Haworth Document Delivery Service [1-800-342-9678, 9:00 a.m. - 5:00 p.m. (EST)].

When television was first introduced, it was not an instant success. The cost of the viewing unit was exorbitant and it was not clear that television would displace movie theaters as the entertainment media of choice. Once it became obvious that television was a medium that was here to stay conflict arose over whether existing movie rights encompassed television rights. The conflict posed the copyright owner against the licensee. Licensees of movie rights argued that their licenses included the right to show the licensed movie over television. Copyright owners countered that television was a new medium and that use of a movie license to broadcast for television exceeded the scope of the license grant. As we shall see, whether the movie license was deemed to include television broadcast had less to do with copyright policy and more to do with contract interpretation. In the present day, as copyright enters the on-line digital world, we are about to re-encounter these same questions and issues.

Before diving into the issues which on-line copyright presents, it is worth noting that copyright law has changed in two significant ways that affect the adjudication of owner's and licensee's rights since the 1909 Copyright Act, the act under which the television cases arose. First, the 1976 Copyright Amendment requires that a transfer of copyright interests–including an exclusive license–be in writing.[4] However, the law leaves open the possibility of a non-exclusive license, which can be oral or even implied by conduct.[5] Second, when the United States joined the Berne Convention, notice requirements involved in obtaining a valid copyright were changed. No longer is it sufficient to verify copyright ownership by searching for the obligatory © symbol. Under Berne, copyright ownership arises automatically at the time of creation, without regard to notice or registration. Indeed, under the 1976 Act, notice requirements were further relaxed relative to the 1909 Act. Under the 1909 Act, a technical default in the copyright notice, such as an incorrect date or author, was sufficient to invalidate the copyright registration.[6] Without proper notice or registration under the 1909 Act, there was no copyright; thus the work was effectively placed in the public domain.[7] Under the current copyright act it is still important to register the work, since certain benefits only accrue upon registration. First, an author or licensee can not obtain statutory damages or attorney's fees without registering.[8] Second, a registered copyright carries a presumption of validity for the copyrighted work.[9] Even without registration, a copyright does not fall into the public domain for lack of proper notice, because notice is no longer a formal prerequisite of copyright ownership.[10] With these facts in mind, an analysis of implied licenses and the scope of existing licenses applied to new on-line media is now possible.

With the end of the second millennia approaching, industrialized society is entering a new world of information and entertainment distribution. The general purpose National Information Infrastructure (NII) is providing electronic access to more and more users in the home and the office. The predecessor of the NII, the Internet, had long been used by academics and some high technology corporations, but the informal nature and relative obscurity of the system left most commercial organizations uninterested in this form of electronic distribution. Yet the initial disinterest is changing and with that change two significant copyright issues arise. First, there is the issue of the copyright status of all the information or "content" that is already available on the NII. Second, there is the issue of whether licenses granted for existing print media encompass distribution in electronic form.

COPYRIGHT STATUS OF WORKS ON THE NII

Since the U.S. joined the Berne Convention, copyright arises at the moment of creation of the work and fixation in a tangible media.[11] For the purpose of copyright infringement of the reproduction right, the copy of the protected work must also be created in a fixed and tangible media. The first question is whether an electronic instance of a work exists in a "tangible media." Certainly works that are physically resident on computer disk drives qualify as "fixed in a tangible media."[12] However, many works on the NII are accessed without creating traditional fixed copies, hence a copyright violation would arguably not occur. Functionally, works can be viewed or browsed via on-line services, such as CompuServe, America On-line, Prodigy, and the World Wide Web (WWW) without creating a traditional "fixation" because the copy only resides temporarily in Random Access Memory (RAM).[13]

Several recent cases have examined the issue regarding whether a RAM copy constitutes "fixation" for copyright purposes. The 9th Circuit Federal Court of Appeals[14] and a federal district judge from the Eastern District of Virginia[15] have both concluded that an operating system residing in RAM–as long as the computer was powered on–was sufficiently "fixed" for copyright purposes. Although the Eastern District clearly stated that some RAM copies would be too transient to constitute fixation,[16] it declined to establish this boundary. Relying on these two cases, the Patent and Trademark Office working group on technology[17] concluded that "it is established law" that all RAM copies are sufficiently fixed for copyright purposes.[18] As numerous commentators have remarked, the proceeding assertion is far from established.[19] Thus it is not clear whether viewing electronic copies infringes the copyright owners' exclusive right to make reproductions of the work or to distribute the work. What is clear is that any electronic work that has an initial fixation, such as on a computer disk drive, is copyrightable.

Even though the author has a copyright, if the author places the work on the NII, some license has certainly been granted. The question of the scope and extent of this implied license is the critical issue facing many publishers at this time. This problem occurs not only in accessing NII materials, but also in routine publishing arrangements, such as newspapers and magazines, that are now going "on-line." For example, does the copyright license from an author for print media include electronic distribution? Further, do voluntary submissions, such as letters to the editor, carry an implied license to distribute electronically? The answers to these questions can critically affect the cost of publishing an electronic edition of a newspaper or magazine.[20] Determining the scope and the nature of a license involves both copyright law and contract law principles.

This document focuses on two important copyright issues for on-line publishers, implied licenses and rules of interpretation for existing licenses. The first section discusses implied licenses. The purpose of this section on implied licenses is to provide some general guidelines for publishers that cannot obtain an express written license for material they need to use. Since copyright infringement is a strict liability statute,[21] it is always preferable to obtain a written agreement, however, written permission is not always feasible. Therefore a general understanding of how to determine whether an implied license exists is useful.

The second section is directed to licensors of existing materials that may be considering on-line publication. If the existing license does not expressly grant a publication right over electronic media, what may the license holder infer from the existing license? In general such determinations are fact specific and involve principles of contract law rather than copyright law, however, some aspects of these decisions are particular to copyright law. A general discussion of contract law and principles is beyond the scope of this document, hence, this section focuses on the aspects of law that are particular to copyright cases.

IMPLIED LICENSE

Although a copyright assignment must be in writing,[22] a non-exclusive implied license may be granted orally or arise from the licensee's conduct.[23] The Court looks at various factors to determine whether a license exists. Courts have considered various factors including, but not limited to:

1. Delivery of the materials.
2. Sophistication of the parties.
3. Other business relations between the parties.

DELIVERY OF MATERIALS

The first factor, delivery of materials, is perhaps most relevant to the electronic publishing world. If someone submits an article or letter for publication to an entity in the business of publishing, delivery itself may create the implied license. In one case, Effects v. Cohen,[24] a special effects firm delivered film footage to a movie producer without a written copyright assignment. Cohen, the producer, used the footage in a distributed film. When business relations turned sour, Effects sued Cohen for copyright infringement. The court wrote that a nonexclusive license may arise by implication where the creator of a work at a defendant's request "hand[s] it over, intending that defendant copy and distribute it."[25] Delivery of a copy of the creation "is one factor that may be relied upon in determining that an implied license has been granted."[26]

SOPHISTICATION OF PARTIES

A second factor that Courts examine to determine the effect of a license is the sophistication of the parties. Courts have long used sophistication of the parties to determine whether undue influence has been exerted by the dominant party. It is also the case that sophistication of the parties may enter in to the issue of contract interpretation.[27] Under the doctrine of "contra proferentem"[28] the interpretation that is less favorable to the party that drafted the term is the interpretation Courts will usually select.[29]

Sophistication of the parties may arise as an issue in license interpretation for copyrights more frequently since the parties are often a publisher or producer (sophisticated) and an individual author (unsophisticated). An example of this principle is Rey v. Lafferty.[30]

In Rey the Court was called upon to untangle a web of license agreements, investment agreements, and conduct between a number of parties to determine whether an implied license to publish a derivative work in book form existed. The facts of Rey are complicated but important to the holding of the case. In the 1940s the plaintiff, Rey, had written a set of books in which she created a fictional monkey named "Curious George." In 1977 Rey entered into a licensing agreement to produce 104 television programs featuring Curious George; Rey also agreed to consider licensing ancillary products rights as well.[31] Not unexpectedly, as with most film projects, there were delays and cost overruns that necessitated renegotiation. After a second round of financing, the films were completed and in 1983 Rey entered into an ancillary products agreement (APA) that granted rights in derivative products for 5 years, subject to Rey's approval.[32] The APA was terminated by Rey on April 10, 1989; however, additional books were produced and published from the 104 films until 1990.[33] Videotapes were also produced and sold.

The licensee argued that the books and videotapes were covered under the original agreement to produce films for television viewing.[34] The Court declined to hold that the original license for the television films included the derivative works of books and videos. The Court relied in part on the ambiguity of the license, but also found that "Rey, an elderly woman, does not appear to have participated in its drafting, and, indeed, does not appear to have been represented by counsel during the larger part of the transaction."[35] The lack of Rey's sophistication relative to the sophistication of the investors ("a professional investment firm accustomed to licensing agreements"[36]), factored against the investment firm in the Courts' determination of whether the license for "television viewing" encompassed an implied license to create derivative works based on the television films.[37]

BUSINESS RELATIONS

A third factor Courts have considered in implied licenses is the business relationship between the parties. In Oddo v. Ries,[38] the Court considered whether a joint partner in a partnership could be held liable for copyright infringement by another partner. In this case Oddo and Ries had formed a partnership to produce a book based on Oddo's previous articles about car repair.[39] Oddo and Ries had a falling out and Ries hired a third party to complete the book. Oddo then sued Ries for copyright infringement.[40] There was no express agreement regarding whether Oddo had given Ries a license to use the preexisting articles. However, the Court held that Oddo, by entering into the partnership, had given the partnership an implied license to use the articles. Otherwise, reasoned the Court, Oddo's contribution to the partnership would have been minimal.[41]

The fact that one party fails to obtain a written transfer of the copyright often puts the Court in the position of trying to do equity to the party that has invested time and labor to bring a work to market when there has been a falling out with the authors. In the case of Pamfiloff v. Giant,[42] Pamfiloff, the complaining party, produced a set of songs which the performing artists subsequently produced with another record company. The original producer, Pamfiloff, had failed to cement the business relationship with a signed written transfer of the reproduction and distribution rights of the songs from the recording artists.[43] Thus, Pamfiloff had no ownership interests in the copyrighted songs. The Court concluded that Pamfiloff did have an implied license to distribute the recorded songs since without such a license, the plaintiff had no means by which to recuperate its investment.[44] In this context Court's presume that the existence of a business relationship is evidence that the parties intended to jointly exploit the work.

SCOPE OF THE LICENSE

In absence of an express grant to publish electronically, the interpretation of the scope of the license determines whether the licensor can go forward with republishing on the new media or risks a copyright infringement suit. In addition to general contract principles such as intent of the parties and "contra proferentem,"[45] there are two generally held views on interpreting whether the scope of the license includes a new use. Nimmer–the leading commentator on copyright law–proposes the preferred method that absence contrary intent by the parties "the licensee may properly pursue any uses which may reasonably be said to fall within the medium as described in the license."[46] The alternate interpretation, "is to assume that a license of rights in a given medium . . . includes only such uses as fall within the unambiguous core meaning of the term . . . and excludes any uses which lie within the ambiguous penumbra."[47]

Courts are divided on which interpretation to use,[48] such division making the publisher's task difficult. However, it is essential to determine the scope of a license, implied or otherwise, since a licensee who exceeds the scope of the license is liable to the author for copyright violation.[49] Once the Court has selected a method for interpreting the license from the above two alternatives, the Court must then determine whether the new use fits within the scope of the license. To make this determination Courts apply general contract law principles with a few nuances that are particular to copyright law.

One key factor is whether a future technology clause exists in the license. A future technology clause grants rights to the licensee regardless of the technology employed to enjoy the work. In Platinum v. Lucasfilm,[50] Platinum sued Lucasfilm for breach of contract, contending that Lucasfilm had exceeded the scope of its license by distributing *American Graffiti* on video disk and cassettes when Lucasfilm was only licensed to distribute

for movie theaters.[51] The Court held that the grant to "exhibit, exploit, market and perform [the work] perpetually throughout the world by any means or method now or hereafter known" was broad enough to cover the new distribution means.[52] The Court found the future grant clause highly probative in determining whether the new technology, video cassettes, was intended to be included in the license grant.

In another case, Cohen v. Paramount,[53] the Court reached the opposite conclusion and prevented the licensee from distributing the work on the new media. Cohen sued Paramount for copyright infringement when Paramount distributed a film on video cassette that included one of Cohen's songs. Paramount originally licensed the song for the motion picture medium. The Cohen contract contained an express reservation of rights to the artist, and lacked a future technology grant.[54] The Court reasoned the artist has not granted distribution rights on future media since there was no future grant clause and the artist expressly reserved all other rights. The Court also observed that it would "frustrate the purpose of the [Copyright] Act" to construe the limited grant as covering new media.[55]

However, a future technology grant is not always dispositive to the question of whether a new technology is covered under an existing license. The Court may interpret a future technology grant in a narrow fashion, thus limiting the applicability of the grant. For example, in Tele-Pac v. Grainer[56] a contract dispute arose over the distribution of motion pictures. The license granted distribution over broadcast media by "any other similar device now known or hereafter to be made known,"[57] but the Court interpreted the grant not to cover the video cassette medium since they are not "broadcast media."[58]

Courts may also consider whether the new use was known at the time the contract was formed. If the use was known, then as Judge Friendly stated, "If the words are broad enough to cover the new use, it seems fairer that the burden of drafting and negotiating an exception should fall on the grantor."[59] If the use was not known or not actively exploited, and there is no future grant clause, Courts will turn to other indicators to resolve the dispute. Such indicators include: The intent of the parties (e.g., General Mills v. Filmtel[60] remanding to the lower Court to determine the intent of the parties to determine if cable broadcast rights were included in a television broadcast license grant when cable television was known but not exploited at the time of the license grant); and sophistication of the parties (e.g., ABKCO v. Westminster[61] where the Court held a 1966 contract granting all rights included the rights in video cassettes even though they were not then known since both parties were sophisticated music publishers[62]). Yet ultimately determining the scope of a license grant turns primarily on contract law doctrines.

CONCLUSION

For existing licensees about to surf into the on-line world the best course of action is to clarify the license with a written instrument executed by the copyright owner. While this may delay entry into the market temporarily, risking copyright litigation and alienating the copyright owner is the alternative. In addition, publishers who build relationships with authors by acknowledging the unique attributes of on-line publishing will benefit from the stronger alliances they forge. The Writers Union has already proposed guidelines for dealing with on-line self-publishing[63]; other industries are certain to follow.

NOTES

1. L. Ray Patterson "The Exclusive 'Right' of Authors," 1 J. Intell. Prop. L. (1994) - discussing the history of the copyright law from the English Statute of Anne to the drafting of the U.S. Constitution Art I §8 and concluding that the purpose of the copyright provision is to provide incentive to authors to bring their works to the public.
2. 17 U.S.C. §106 (1994)
3. 17 U.S.C. §201(d)(1)
4. 17 U.S.C. §204(a)
5. Nimmer & D. Nimmer, "Copyright" §10.03[A] 10-38 and fn. 19 (1994)
6. 17 U.S.C. §10 (1909)
7. 17 U.S.C. §14 (1909)
8. 17 U.S.C. §412 (1994)
9. 17 U.S.C. §410(c)
10. 17 U.S.C. 408(a)
11. 17 U.S.C. 101
12. Id.
13. Whether the copy actually resides only in RAM or is temporarily copied to disk is a function of the software. Rather than debate the technical issues of how the software works, all browsing software is categorized functionally. Thus browsing is characterized by RAM copies and downloading is characterized by disk copies.
14. MIA vs. Corp. v. Peak Computers, 991 F.2d 511,26 U.S.P.Q.2d (9th Cir. 1993) cert denied 114 S.Ct. 671(1994)
15. Advanced Computers Sys. v. MAI 845 F.Supp. 356 (E.D. Va. 1994)
16. Id. at 363

17. Intellectual Property and the National Information Infrastructure: A preliminary Draft of the Report of the Working Group on Intellectual Property Rights, U.S. Patent & Trademark Office, July 1994 (hereafter Green Paper)

18. Green Paper at line 926

19. R. Katz & J. Arnold, "An Unprecedented Opinion With Sparse Analysis," Computer Law, (1993); K. Levin "MAI v. Peak: Should Loading Operating System Software into RAM Constitute Copyright Infringement?," 24 Golden Gate U.L. Rev. 649 (1994); R. Goff, "Can Software Copyrights Restrict Related Competition?," 11 No. 10 Computer Law, 9 (1994); 'T. Arriola "Software Copyright Infringement Claims after MAI Systems v. Peak Computer," 69 Wash. L. Rev. 405(1994); J. Litman "The Exclusive Right to Read," 13 Cardozo Arts & Ent. L.J. 29(1994); P. Samuelson "Legally Speaking," Communication of the ACM Dec. 1994 pg. 25; S. Orenstein, "9th Circuit: You Can Fix, But You Better Not Touch," Recorder (1993)

20. For example, a newspaper may have a license to use copyrighted works in a particular edition, e.g., daily, weekend, or Sunday. For an electronic work to constitute the same edition as the pulp version it must contain all of the same features and columns. Thus the inability to obtain one electronic license could invalidate other licenses.

21. 17 U.S.C. §501 provides that anyone who violates one of the author's exclusive rights is liable for copyright infringement.

22. 17 U.S.C. 204(a)

23. Nimmer & D. Nimmer, "Copyright" §10.03[A] 10-38 and fn. 19 (1994)

24. Effects Assocs. Inc. v. Cohen 908 F.2d 555 (9th Cir. 1990) cert denied 498 U.S. 1103 (1991)

25. Id. at 558

26. Id. at 559 fn. 6

27. Farnsworth, "Contracts" §4.17; See for example, Gulf Oil Corp. v. American Louisiana Pipe Line Co. 282 F.2d 401(6th Cir. 1960). Different language in two sections held not to be inadvertent because the contract was drafted by lawyers.

28. meaning–against the profferer–the contract doctrine that an ambiguous contract term will be interpreted against the drafter.

29. Farnsworth §7.11

30. Rey v. Lafferty 26 U.S.P.Q2d 1339,990 F.2d 1379(1st Cir. 1993) cert denied 114 S.Ct. 94,126 L.Ed.2d 61(1993)

31. Id. at 1381

32. Id. at 1382

33. Id.

34. Id. at 1389-90

35. Id. at 1391

36. Id.

37. See Ettore v. Philco Television Broadcasting Corp., 229 F.2d 481 (3rd Cir. 1956), cert denied 351 U.S. 926(1956) relying on the fact that Ettore was a prizefighter, not a business person, in determining the scope of a license.

38. Oddo v. Ries 743 F.2d 630,222 U.S.P.Q. 799 (9th Cir. 1984)
39. Id. at 632
40. Id.
41. Id. at 634
42. Pamfiloff v. Giant Records Inc. 794 F.Supp 933 (N.D.Ca. 1992)
43. Id. at 934
44. Id. at 938-39
45. See note 27 supra
46. Nimmer §10.10[B]
47. Id. at 10-92 fn. 17
48. Following Nimmer; Bartsch v. Metro-Goldwyn-Mayer, Inc. 391 F.2d 150 (2nd Cir 1968) cert. denied 393 U.S. 826 (1968); Rooney v. Columbia Pictures Industries Inc. 538 F.Supp 211 (S.D.N.Y. 1982) aff'd 714 F.2d 117 (2nd Cir. 1982) cert. denied 460 U.S. 1984,103 S.Ct. 1774,76 L.Ed.2d (1983).
49. MacLean Assocs., Inc. v. Wm. M. Mercer-Meridinger-Hansen, Inc. 952 F.2d 769,779 (3rd Cir. 1991). Licensee who exceeds the scope of the license may be liable for copyright infringement.
50. Platinum Record Co. v. Lucasfilm, Ltd. 566 F.Supp 226 (D.N.J. 1983)
51. Id. at 227 (It is noteworthy that Platinum did not include a copyright infringement claim since the facts of the case would have supported such a claim).
52. Id.
53. Cohen v. Paramount Pictures Corp. 845 F.2d 851(9th Cir. 1988)
54. Id. at 855
55. Id. at 854
56. Tele-Pac, Inc. v. Grainer 168 A.D.2d 11,570 N.Y.S.2d 521(1st Dep't 1991)
57. Id. at 524-25
58. Id.
59. Bartsch v. Metro-Goldwyn-Mayer, Inc. 391 F.2d 150,155 (2nd Cir 1968)
60. General Mills, Inc. v. Filmtel Int'l Corp. 599 N.Y.S.2d (1993)
61. ABKCO Music, Inc. v. Westminster Music, Ltd. 838 F.Supp 153 (S.D.N.Y 1993)
62. Id. at 157
63. http://www.nlighting.com/e-money.html

Copyright: Economic Rights and Moral Rights

John Cox

Among a collection of papers on legal issues affecting the rights of publishers and their customers there should be an analysis of the practical effects of the law on the rights and duties of both stakeholders. Nowhere is this more necessary than in the area of intellectual property. This paper is concerned with the business applications of modern copyright law in one segment of the knowledge industry: academic and scholarly publishing.

The history of modern copyright law can be traced back to the invention of printing. In England, it originated as a method by which the Crown controlled the licensing of authors, booksellers, printers and publishers. In France the notion of copyright was developed as a means of protecting authors' rights in works that might otherwise be appropriated, misrepresented or distorted by others. Only in the early 18th century did English law start to concern itself with the rights of authors and with copyright as a property right, with the Statute of Anne in 1709. These two elements of principle are important to the understanding of copyright law; they have converged into a system that recognizes the rights of the creator of a work and provides the means by which he or she may exercise control over its use. After the Statute of Anne, other European countries adopted copyright laws, amongst others Denmark in 1741, France in 1793, Spain in 1847 and Germany in 1870. The first US Federal Copyright Act was passed in 1790.

John Cox, OBE, BA (Oxon), Barrister-at-Law, FInstD, MInstM, is MCIT Managing Director, Carfax Publishing Company, P. O. Box 25, Abingdon, Oxfordshire OX14 3UE, UK.

[Haworth co-indexing entry note]: "Copyright: Economic Rights and Moral Rights." Cox, John. Co-published simultaneously in *The Acquisitions Librarian* (The Haworth Press, Inc.) No. 15, 1996, pp. 123-128; and: *Current Legal Issues in Publishing* (ed: A. Bruce Strauch) The Haworth Press, Inc., 1996, pp. 123-128. Single or multiple copies of this article are available from The Haworth Document Delivery Service [1-800-342-9678, 9:00 a.m. - 5:00 p.m. (EST)].

Although modern copyright law is a feature of national law, it is generally based around the provisions of the Berne Convention for the Protection of Literary and Artistic Works. Over 90 countries are signatories to Berne, which provides for both minimum standards of protection and for the reciprocal recognition and enforcement that enables publishers and other merchants of intellectual property to trade on a global basis.

Copyright law is a tradeable property right. The owner of the copyright can not only issue copies of the work himself to the public, but also license others to do the same, or indeed refuse to permit others. Copying includes photocopying, transcribing, microfilming, or converting into machine readable form. The law protects not only scholarly work, but literature, dramatic works, music, artistic work, sound recordings, films and broadcasts.

Copyright is important to publishers and authors alike. As traders in intellectual property, publishers have to obtain an economic return on the investment they make in their products. They add value to the information originally created by the author; it is that added value which publishers expect customers to pay for. The principles of ownership and control underlying copyright provide the legal basis on which publishers conduct their business.

From the publishers' point of view, copyright is an economic issue rather than a legal issue. The dominance of the United States in creative works–book publishing and movie making–and in other forms of intellectual property is due in large part to the rigorous enforcement of US copyright law by the Courts. The United Kingdom, another substantial exporter of intellectual property, is equally rigorous in its approach. Copyright law serves not only publishers but record companies, television broadcasters and, not least, the film industry. The copyright system is intended to encourage creativity by permitting the originators of works to profit from their endeavors.

For publishers, the challenges to copyright law being expressed in the scholarly community reinforce the view that what is at stake is economics rather than the principles underlying the law. Research funding doubled during the 15 years from 1975 to 1990. The output of research articles and monographs also doubled.[1] But academic library expenditure increased by only 40%.[2] The response of some librarians, burdened by the twin problems of inadequate budgets and an information explosion, has been to challenge the organization and management of copyright that has been established for a generation, perhaps in the hope that the use of electronic media may somehow weaken or even evade the application of copyright law. Indeed, the electronic age has made it more difficult to protect copyright and to trace its breaches. Nevertheless, this challenge is by no means supported by their faculty colleagues or by the learned societies of which most are members.

The process of publishing remains essential to the selection, presentation and packaging of scholarly information. Publishing brings an orderly and rational infrastructure to the output of scholarly endeavor. Authors receive a reward for the exploitation of their works by publishers, either in the form of a royalty on sales revenue or in the indirect benefits that accrue to an author from being published in a journal of repute that is efficiently targeted and presented to its intended market. That authors of scholarly papers seeking publication in the journal of their choice assign their copyright for no fee to publishers does not in law degrade the value of the property right possessed by the publisher; whether this right is exercised in printed or in electronic form makes no difference to the principle. The law is needed to continue to balance the needs of users for access to and exchange of information with the rights of authors and publishers to financial benefit.

The electronic media have opened up a new range of possibilities and problems. Authors are the source of important and authoritative information. They expect publication to be prompt and location of their material to be easy; it must not be lost in the uncoordinated noise of the Internet. They continue to rely on publishers to provide an imprint or name that certifies the quality of the work, delivers a well-produced product and protects their interests by placing the imprint on that work to distinguish it from the mass of informal information and gossip that is otherwise available. A publisher will be seen less as a producer of print products, and more as a provider of intellectual property distributed in the medium that best suits the nature of the individual work and the needs of the readership.

"Publication" must, in the future, include availability and distribution on-line from a database; only by doing so will a measure of economic protection be provided to the publisher. In the electronic environment "publication" may also mean that a publisher declares an author's work acceptable by placing it in a database as the definitive copy of that work. In consequence, transmission of a copyright work through a computer network must be regarded as a form of copying. It has the same effect as making a photocopy. The recipient of a copyright work is simply not free to copy it and pass it on without the owner's permission, unless already licensed to do so.

On-line publishing has the potential to create genuine interaction between author and reader. Readers can attach comments to a work, and authors can reply. It is important we develop protocols to ensure that these comments do not corrupt or alter the original. By posting such comments, the authors are formally attaching them to the published work as part of a public discussion. The comments themselves should not be altered or withdrawn without formal annotation on the database.

It is in this developing electronic environment that the value of "moral rights" becomes most obvious. Moral rights originated in France; the original principle underlying French copyright law was always concerned with the rights of authors: not only economic rights but also the right to have the personal relationship between a creator and his or her work recognized at law. Moral rights are now generally applied throughout the European community, and were incorporated into UK law in the Copyright Designs and Patents Act 1988.

Moral rights provide a set of mechanisms to protect published works from alterations without review and approval by the author. In principle, the policies and practices of any ethical publisher should already take account of authors' rights. In practice, the too frequent occurrence of plagiarism, and the ease with which material can be adapted and used by others using modern technology points to the need for the legal protection of the author.

Moral rights in UK law comprise:

1. The right to be identified as the author–or the director of a film–in respect of any work issued to or to be performed or exhibited in public.[3] This right of *paternity* does not exist unless it is asserted in accordance with the statute.[4] Its duration is the same as that of copyright, and it adheres to the author whether the author continues to own the copyright itself or has assigned or licensed that to others. The right of paternity does not apply to anything done with a copyright owner's authority where copyright is first vested in the author's employer. Neither does it apply to newspaper or magazine articles, news reports or computer programs.
2. The right to *integrity*: the right of objection to derogatory treatment of the work.[5] "Derogatory" treatment means distortion or mutilation or any action prejudicial to the honor or reputation of the author. The word "treatment" is defined as including translations, alterations and adaptations of the work. The same exceptions apply as to the paternity right.
3. The right of *non-attribution*: the right not to have a work falsely attributed to an author.[6] This right lasts for the lifetime of the author plus 20 years only.
4. The right of a person commissioning a copyright photograph not to have copies issued to the public or exhibited or broadcast. This right subsists for the duration of copyright. This is known as the right of *disclosure*. Under French law, it is somewhat more broadly drawn.

It is important to note that moral rights are not transferable or assignable. This applies even though the author may have assigned copyright in the work, say, to the publisher. However, they can be waived in writing. Breach of moral rights is an infringement that is actionable as a breach of statutory duty owed to the person entitled to the right, and will normally result in the award of damages.

The "balance" between the rights of author and publisher on the one hand and the user on the other must be a matter, eventually, for the courts. How it is struck will affect what sort of information products publishers and other information providers are willing to invest in creating and distributing. The effectiveness of the legal means available to protect works from illicit use or distortion is no less critical for the future of publishers than the development of security and encryption technologies to protect information accessible on-line. Indeed, this is already recognized in the United States by the High Performance Computing Act, 1991; the Network (NREN) should be designed and operated to ensure the continued application of the law of copyright.[7]

Many database publishers already seek to avoid the uncertainties of copyright law, particularly in the ill-defined area of fair use, by granting access to their products in the form of license agreements. Indeed, the agreement of specific contractual provisions in relation to the use of intellectual property rights brings greater certainty and understanding both to publisher and to customer. Such licenses could conceivably so restrict libraries' ability to supply copies of works either to their patrons or to other libraries on inter-library loan that the freedom previously enjoyed under fair use would become meaningless. This publisher believes that is unlikely, as contracts cannot bind third parties. But those same contracts can certainly restrict fair use, throwing the onus onto the customer to rely on the provisions of local law on the enforceability of unfair contractual terms.

Any reasonable and successful publisher must enable authors to communicate with the widest possible relevant audience, must represent authors in disseminating their scholarship and protecting their interests, must ensure that all information published meets the required standards for quality, presentation, authority and originality, and must assist readers in locating the information they need. The publishers' continuing role is to add value to raw information, package it and deliver it in an orderly manner. Copyright law continues to provide the best–indeed the only–regime where information providers are able to protect their investments of time, skill and finance. The issue, as ever, is not one of legal principle but of economic balance.

REFERENCES

1. *Science and Engineering Indicators, 1991 edition, National Science Board.* SCISEARCH data from ISI, 1975-91
2. R&D: *Science and Engineering Indicators,* 1991, National Science Board; Library Expenditure: Association of Research Libraries (ARL) Statistics.
3. Copyright Designs & Patents Act 1988, UK, Section 77
4. ibid, Section 78
5. ibid, Section 80
6. ibid, Section 84
7. 15 U. S. C. § 5512 (c) (5) (1991): *the Act also requires continued application of laws relating to national security and to access to databases.*

Facilitating Copyrights: The Role of the Middleman

Rebecca T. Lenzini
Ward Shaw

The goal of all parties participating in the information creation and usage chain is to make information available as cheaply, easily and conveniently as possible. The challenge is to find reasonable and effective ways to observe copyright in the process. To the user or buyer, we must be as unobtrusive as possible, not interfering or slowing in any way the speed or ease with which that individual is able to obtain the desired information, yet still allowing the rights holder the opportunity to set policy regarding his or her material and to obtain a reasonable fee.

These goals are not different from those we embrace within a print environment where we work with existing copyright mechanisms. The fact is that copyright as we know it works rather well in the print on paper world. It remains relatively difficult to copy anything of any size, so existing copyright mechanisms have provided and still provide reasonably effective legal protection against cases of outright stealing and republication. (The success of the publishing industry in the Kinko's case provides evidence of the effectiveness of the existing copyright law in relation to paper-based systematic distribution.)

The challenge is different, however, with the advent of electronic systems and particularly with the emergence of worldwide networks, thanks

---

Rebecca T. Lenzini is President of CARL Corporation, and has published numerous articles on journal pricing, document delivery, library cooperation and automation. Ward Shaw is Chairman and CEO of CARL Corporation, and serves on the Network Advisory Committee of the Library of Congress.

Address correspondence to: CARL Systems, 3801 E. Florida Avenue, Number 300, Denver, CO 80210.

[Haworth co-indexing entry note]: "Facilitating Copyrights: The Role of the Middleman." Lenzini, Rebecca T. and Ward Shaw. Co-published simultaneously in *The Acquisitions Librarian* (The Haworth Press, Inc.) No. 15, 1996, pp. 129-133; and: *Current Legal Issues in Publishing* (ed: A. Bruce Strauch) The Haworth Press, Inc., 1996, pp. 129-133. Single or multiple copies of this article are available from The Haworth Document Delivery Service [1-800-342-9678, 9:00 a.m. - 5:00 p.m. (EST)].

in large part to the ease of copying which these new technologies have introduced. With personal computers, fax machines, scanners and networks, it is relatively straightforward to invent systems that have the effect of enabling institutions and individuals to avoid purchasing published hard copies of various documents, and instead to obtain them electronically.

From a strictly economic point of view, the arguments for technology are strong, particularly in the area of scholarly publishing. Andrew Odlyzko (Odlyzko), in his article "Tragic loss or good riddance? The impending demise of traditional scholarly journals," provides an analysis of the improvements in pure data storage capability which, according to his calculations, will allow the text of all the 50,000 mathematical papers published each year to be stored in 2.5 gigabytes at a cost in the hundreds, not thousands, of dollars. As he notes " . . . it is already possible to store all the current mathematical publications at an annual cost much less than that of the subscription to a single journal."

Furthermore, Odlyzko does not base his arguments for the electronic options purely upon economics; more important to this scholar/author is the interactive nature of electronic publications, which he believes will serve to improve the quality of scholarship. And he notes the obvious convenience factors which electronic mechanisms will provide, allowing round the clock access to information from the researcher's home or office.

Publishers, according to Karen Hunter of Elsevier Science Publishers (Hunter), are developing strategies for utilizing the new technologies and are working as rapidly as possible to convert present products to electronic form. The goal for publishers is to add value through electronic enhancements and to create new products by clustering and tailoring existing information to new market segments and individuals.

Reflecting the view of the commercial publisher, Hunter has identified pricing as the single biggest challenge ahead and has noted the growing interest among publishers in licensing arrangements, which will allow published materials to be widely distributed and used, yet will compensate the publisher. In her words, what is sought are " . . . appropriate compromises between user access and publisher security" (Hunter, 32).

Hunter is certainly correct to identify issues of economics as dominant in this area. In the print on paper environment, the publisher willingly sells a library a subscription to a journal, knowing that many people may share its use in that library, but also knowing that it is relatively inconvenient to use the journal in the library. In the electronic environment, that same publisher will be willing to sell the same journal in electronic form, but not at anything like the same price, because use is likely to be high since it is convenient for many people to use.

Of course, the problem is that not many copyright fees were collected in the old environment. The role of copyright was, practically, that of protection, and real money changed hands largely surrounding large deals relating to republication in different forms, markets, and the like, and certainly not on an individual transactional basis. The copyright legislation, the case law, the mechanisms for payment (or lack thereof), and most importantly, the general perception did not evolve to enable, control, and protect a marketplace of individual article uses and attendant copyright payments associated with those individual uses.

However, individual article use is exactly what is rapidly evolving today, driven by technology (we can do it), economics (it costs less), and convenience (users demand it). In order to support this evolution, a new set of mechanisms and expectations is needed, which allows the easy and normal collection of copyright fees directly from end users (or their institutions) whenever copies are distributed to them. Ideally this same mechanism will also allow the easy and normal payment of copyright fees to rightsholders based on the number of copies, distributions, or uses of their works. It is worth noting that each of these transactions is likely to be quite small in dollars, but that the number of transactions can be assumed to be very high. The copyright system, therefore, must add to its role of protection a new role–that of providing significant compensation to rightsholders.

To add this new role, we must find ways to make copyright easy to understand, easy to account, easy to administer, and easy to change. It must be easy to understand because we cannot afford to go to court every time a question arises. It must be easy to account to ensure rapid and economical processing of large numbers of transactions. It must be easy to administer for the same reasons. And it must be easy to change because the technology, the system itself, and marketplace demands are changing very rapidly, and they drive the requirements of this new role of copyright.

One solution to this transformation already lies in the technology that creates the issue in the first place. Today much of the network distribution of documents originates from middlemen, that is, organizations or database services which provide indexes to information with delivery options. These delivery options range from photocopies mailed to the user, to images faxed over phone lines or downloaded over the networks, to full text which appears on screen for local printing or downloading.

These middlemen are already collecting the data which is required to make per transaction copyright observance possible and even easy. For example, it is possible for network based servers which house or index documents for distribution to collect, at the time of document supply, a copyright fee in addition to whatever transaction fee is associated with the distribution itself. It is also not difficult for network based distributors to keep track of items delivered and fees collected, and to amalgamate payments to rightsholders on a regular basis. It is also possible, and reasonably easy, subject to constraints of privacy, to provide to rightsholders considerable statistical information about the use of their works.

While the computing for this transaction based copyright system is relatively trivial, there are a number of associated issues which must be addressed in a larger context. The first issue is who to pay, that is, who is the rightsholder? In order for the system to work on a transaction basis, middlemen must know unequivocally who they should pay for each copy distributed–whether it be the publisher, the author, the author's employer, an RRO such as the Copyright Clearance Center, or an organization such as the National Writer's Union which represents authors. Further, the middleman must not become a party to the resolution of any questions or disputes among potential claimants involved, because he is acting simply as collector and payer as far as copyright is concerned.

A second issue is that it must be very clear how much the copyright fee is, and there must be a "level playing field." Each deliverer or distributor should be required to pay the same amount for the delivery of any given document, and to the same rightsholder. Further, this needs to be international in scope, since networks are also international in scope. A distributor in country A delivering a document to a purchaser in country B should pay the same copyright fee as a distributor in country C performing the same delivery.

A third issue relates to trust. The overall collection and payment system needs to be working in order for rightsholders to believe in it enough to commit to it. At the same time, the system needs rightsholders to commit in order to generate the critical mass required to become stable and trustworthy. Today, there are numbers of limited experiments underway designed to test various electronic distribution and payment methods. In fact, our own organizations, CARL and UnCover, are involved in several of these experiments.

Many of these ventures are designed to protect one or another party's economic interest. The experiments are interesting and useful in that they enable the testing of various technologies, but will not shed much light on the fundamental changing paradigm and its effects precisely for the very reason that they are limited and experimental. This problem is a classical one which haunts almost all fundamental transitions, and it will eventually disappear. We note it here as an issue only because it is important to keep in mind when analyzing these various experiments. It is tempting to assume "an answer" based on whichever experiment one likes best, sometimes without a perspective on overall trends.

Even with this caveat, though, the general shape of this transition seems clear. Middlemen will provide colocation and distribution services of individual works, from a variety of rightsholders and a variety of sources, to individual users of those works. As a part of each individual transaction, the middleman distributor will collect a copyright or use fee from the end user on behalf of the rightsholders and will pay the rightsholder. The same electronic technologies that make these new distribution methods work will also enable handling the millions of small economic transactions contemplated in this model. And, as an additional benefit, this new model will open the authoring and communication process to many more people by removing a range of increasingly artificial barriers to traditional publication.

REFERENCES

The authors have used several concepts which were originally presented in "Delivery of Documents and More: A View of Trends Affecting Libraries and Publishers," a paper written and delivered by Rebecca T. Lenzini at the University of Oklahoma Conference on Access, Resource Sharing and Collection Development, March 2-3, 1995.

Hunter, Karen. "The changing business of scholarly publishing," *Journal of Library Administration*, 1993, v.19, no.3/4, pp. 23-38.

Odlyzko, Andrew. "Tragic loss or good riddance? The impending demise of traditional scholarly journals," September 26, 1994. Condensed version to be published in the *Notices of the American Mathematical Society*, January 1995. Full version to be published in *Internal Journal of Human-Computer Studies*, and reprinted in "Electronic Publishing Confronts Academia: The Agenda for the Year 2000," Robin P. Peek and Gregory B. Newby, eds., MIT Press/ASIS Monograph, MIT Press, 1995. (available in full text at ftp://netlib.att.com/netlib/att/math/odlyzko/tragic.loss.Z)

OLD PROBLEMS REMAIN

First Amendment Issues in Publishing

Glen M. Secor

This article is being written and compiled in late April 1995, amidst the emotional and political fallout from the savage bombing of the federal building in Oklahoma City. That early fallout has included allegations, including by President Clinton, that the words of conservative talk show hosts have created an atmosphere which encourages such actions as the Oklahoma City bombing. A variety of other First Amendment controversies have swirled about in recent months.

In January of this year, a California couple was convicted of obscenity charges in a federal court in Tennessee for pictures which were downloaded from the couple's BBS in California. In March, the U.S. Senate Commerce Committee passed the Communications Decency Act of 1995, designed to regulate the flow of obscene materials and the access to indecent material by children online. For months now, the O. J. Simpson trial has both captivated and repulsed the nation, while at the same time gener-

The author may be contacted at the Yankee Book Peddler, 999 Maple Street, Contoocook, NH 03229.

[Haworth co-indexing entry note]: "First Amendment Issues in Publishing." Secor, Glen M. Co-published simultaneously in *The Acquisitions Librarian* (The Haworth Press, Inc.) No. 15, 1996, pp. 135-144; and: *Current Legal Issues in Publishing* (ed: A. Bruce Strauch) The Haworth Press, Inc., 1996, pp. 135-144. Single or multiple copies of this article are available from The Haworth Document Delivery Service [1-800-342-9678, 9:00 a.m. - 5:00 p.m. (EST)].

ating profits for media companies and book publishers. On March 27, *I Want to Tell You* by O. J. Simpson and Laurence Schiller ranked seventh on the *Publishers Weekly* bestselling nonfiction hardcover list. In November 1994, a $200 million defamation suit was filed against the Prodigy Service Company for a posting made to one of Prodigy's online bulletin boards.

In short, we have seen in the past few months a number of major events with First Amendment implications. It appears that issues of free speech and commercial liability for unprotected speech will figure prominently in our political and social debates in the coming months. And while many of the events cited above do not directly involve publishers, it would be a mistake for free speech advocates in the publishing industry to ignore these matters. The volatile political environment of America in the mid-1990s and the growth of online communication will force us, as a society, to examine and balance our commitments to free speech, individual liberty, law enforcement, and public safety. The outcomes of these debates, legislative initiatives, and lawsuits will have profound implications for all of us, including publishers.

This article will briefly examine some First Amendment-related issues which should be of interest to publishers and information professionals.[1]

"SON OF SAM" LAWS

In 1977, New York enacted a crime victimization statute to compensate victims of crime and to prevent criminals from profiting from their crimes.[2] This law was prompted by concern over reports that David Berkowitz, the "Son of Sam" killer, stood to gain handsomely by selling his story to the media. The law as originally drafted was struck down by the U.S. Supreme Court in *Simon & Schuster, Inc. v. Members of the New York State Crime Victims Board*.[3]

While many at the time saw this case as representing a major victory for free speech and publishing, the fact is that the Supreme Court took issue with the way in which the New York legislature sought to achieve its goals, not with the goals themselves. The Court found a compelling state interest in preventing criminals from profiting from their crimes and in compensating the victims of crime. The original New York "Son of Sam" law was flawed because it singled out one type of income, that derived from the sale or telling of the criminal's story, for escrow into a crime victims fund, while ignoring other income and assets of the criminal. Further, it defined a "person convicted of a crime" in an overly broad manner, so as to include those never actually convicted, but who admitted to having committed crimes. For these reasons, the law was deemed to place unconstitutional burdens on free speech and was struck down.

Subsequent to *Simon & Schuster*, New York and a handful of other states amended their crime victimization statutes to remove the unconstitutional burdens on free speech found in *Simon & Schuster*.[4] But while some 45 states have "Son of Sam" laws on the books, only New York, Iowa, Maryland, and Virginia appear to have amended their crime victimization statutes to fully comply with the requirements of *Simon & Schuster*.[5]

The fight over "Son of Sam" laws is moving to California, where the state legislature has taken steps to prevent witnesses and jurors in the O. J. Simpson trial from cashing in on their stories.[6] Further, the California Attorney General has initiated " 'Son of Sam' proceedings" against two convicted criminals, Rodney Acala for writing a book, and Joe Hunt for establishing a 900 number.[7]

How these California cases turn out remains to be seen. The broader issue, one which perhaps cannot be settled by any court other than the court of public opinion, is how we regard the speech of convicted criminals and how we feel about the financial incentives attached to their stories. On the one hand, we seem appalled by the idea of murderers and other criminals profiting from the book and movie rights to their stories. On the other hand, we, as a society, devour these stories, generating the very profits at issue. With the "Son of Sam" laws, we are attempting to have our cake and eat it too, secure in the justification that the profits from book, movie, etc., are going to victim compensation rather than to the criminal.

Yet, it seems apparent from the legislative histories of these laws, including New York's and California's, that the primary goal is not victim compensation, but rather to make sure that the criminal does not profit from the crime. The New York law came into being because state legislators were outraged at reports that David Berkowitz might be able to sell the rights to his story for substantial sums. The fact that the law originally targeted only such profits, and not the other income or assets of the criminal, makes clear the legislative intent. And it seems unlikely that the primary motivation of the California legislature in enacting special "Son of Sam" laws just in time for the O. J. Simpson trial was to provide compensation to the survivors of Nicole Brown Simpson and Ronald Goldman, the murder victims. This is not to say that a goal of preventing the murder defendant from profiting from the story, or preventing financial considerations from influencing jurors or witnesses, would not be worthwhile. We should be honest, though, in recognizing these as the primary goals of the "Son of Sam" laws, not victim compensation.

As is, certain of the California laws go beyond removing the financial incentive from the criminal and actually seek to penalize anyone, including the publisher, involved in bringing a juror or witness story to print.[8] Here the intent seems to be to discourage the very telling of the story; a legislative gag order, if you will.

In this context, we should ask ourselves why, as a society, if we are so opposed to having criminals profit from the telling of their stories, or if we are concerned about financial considerations interfering with the work of our courts, we should need legislation to accomplish these goals. Perhaps, within the supposed free marketplace of ideas, we should just let these stories be told. If consumers knew that some of the profits from the stories of criminals were making their way back to the criminals, perhaps this knowledge would serve to curb our appetite for such things. Or, if that appetite is truly as insatiable as it appears to be, perhaps we should save some of our revulsion at ourselves as consumers, rather than reserving it all for the criminal who sold the story.

Simon & Schuster provided a blueprint for the drafting of a constitutional "Son of Sam" law. Some states have amended their laws to comply with the decision. California has moved beyond the traditional objectives of "Son of Sam" laws by attempting to stifle juror and witness stories. Even if one supports the concept of the "Son of Sam" laws, California has shown us that it is but a small leap from those laws to other laws which choke off certain kinds of speech altogether.

DEFAMATION IN CYBERSPACE: PRODIGY SUED FOR LIBEL

Stratton v. Prodigy[9] appears to be the big online service provider liability case that lawyers and industry experts have been anticipating. Someone posted some very unkind remarks about Stratton Oakmont, Inc., a New York investment bank, in a Prodigy discussion group, accusing Stratton Oakmont and its president of criminal fraud. The post appeared on October 23, 1994 and allegedly remained on the system for 19 days. The poster, whose identity has not yet been determined, used a dormant identification number of someone who had worked at Prodigy three years ago to gain online access. The Prodigy ex-employee, under whose name the defamatory post was made, has apparently been cleared and is due to be released from the suit.

Stratton Oakmont is suing for $200 million, including $100 million in punitive damages. Out of the potential defendants, Prodigy is certainly the one with deep pocket, being jointly owned by IBM and Sears, Roebuck. Stratton Oakmont is arguing that Prodigy has a duty to screen posted messages for defamatory remarks. They further charge that Prodigy was negligent for allowing a hacker to access the ex-employee's old identification number.

From a legal liability standpoint, the issue here is whether Prodigy is a common carrier, simply passing communications along like the phone company, or a private information provider, with responsibility for what appears on its system. Is Prodigy like a bookstore or newsstand, as CompuServe was found to be in a 1991 libel case,[10] or is it more like a publisher, with editorial responsibility and accountability? That Prodigy does do scanning of posted messages, using software to delete posts with profane or offensive language, indicates that they are more than a mere conduit for online communications. Yet, using software to scan for certain dirty words is a bit different than scanning messages for potentially libelous statements. The latter involves a great deal of judgment and probably a tremendous commitment of labor, given that more than 75,000 messages are posted to more than 1,000 Prodigy boards each day.

And what of free speech in cyberspace? Would not massive screening and censoring by online service providers dampen the free exchange of ideas and information that many believe are the raison d'etre of the Net? This is a profound case for all information providers and Net users, including publishers who hope to plan to distribute their content online.

In *Cubby v. CompuServe*, CompuServe's liability, like that of a bookstore or newsstand, was limited to instances in which "it knew or had reason to know" of an allegedly libelous statement and failed to take appropriate action. One would think that a court would be reluctant to impose on Prodigy and other service providers an obligation to screen all message postings for defamatory statements (or statements constituting hate crimes or civil rights violations, or threats upon other people, or . . .), and that the "knew or should have known" standard will be applied in this case. Unless Prodigy actually knew or should have known of the post in question (i.e., if a user had notified Prodigy of a problem in that particular board, with or without specifying the content of the allegedly defamatory message), or unless they are found to have been negligent in leaving the door open for the hacker who posted the message, it appears unlikely that Prodigy will be found liable.

Then again, as so many high profile cases have proven in recent months, predicting the outcome of trials is a dicey proposition. We should watch this case very carefully.

OBSCENITY IN CYBERSPACE: CALIFORNIA BBS OPERATORS CONVICTED IN TENNESSEE

BBS busts seem to come weekly these days, but this case has caused a firestorm among cyber libertarians. Robert and Carleen Thomas operated the Amateur Action BBS from Milpitas, CA. After a postal inspector in Memphis, TN downloaded certain images from the AA-BBS, and after this same inspector mailed a kiddie porn tape to Mr. Thomas, the Thomases were arrested for distribution of obscene material and receipt of child pornography. The child pornography charge did not stick, as the Thomases had not requested that material and were unaware of its shipment until they received it, but the couple was convicted in U.S. District Court on the obscenity charges. On Dec. 2, 1994 Mr. Thomas was sentenced to 3 years and a month in prison, while Mrs. Thomas received two-and-a-half years.

Obscenity is an ill-defined concept in the law, but it is supposed to be based upon *community standards*.[11] Here, the images were downloaded from a database in California to a computer in Tennessee. The trial took place in Tennessee, using the standards of the community in Tennessee to define obscenity. One supposes that the prosecution could have taken place in any of the fifty states, so long as that state is where the images were downloaded. This is an important fact for BBS operators and online information providers: where obscenity is concerned, prosecution can take place anywhere in the U.S., according to the standards of that community.

This case points up the difficulty of fitting existing legal standards and practices, in this case the geography-based community standards test in obscenity cases, into a world of national and international data networks. If this had been a traditional printed obscenity case, at least the Thomases would have taken the affirmative step of mailing the offending materials to Tennessee. Even sending the materials in an email-type transaction to a recipient whose system the sender knows is in Tennessee would be a more positive step than the one taken. A user in Tennessee downloading the files from a database in California hardly seems like an affirmative step by the database owner to distribute the materials in Tennessee.

One other possible "community," in addition to California and Tennessee, exists here–the community of online users who utilize the Internet and BBSs. Perhaps this community is too amorphous to have "standards" which could be used in obscenity cases or other trials, but is that not truly the community whose standards should be used to judge the appropriateness of what is online? Perhaps geographic definitions of "community" are not the most useful in judging acts committed in cyberspace.

OBSCENITY IN CYBERSPACE II: THE COMMUNICATION DECENCY ACT OF 1995 (S.314)

When we talk about the Internet and the future of digital communication, we tend to stress the enormous potential for information sharing.

While we are concerned about the development of digital networks, especially in terms of adequate access for all members of society, most of us are excited about the current explosion of information and the new technologies available for information access.

In cyberspace, though, what one regards as "bad" information can flow just as easily as what one regards as "good" information. This is not unlike the situations which exist with television and radio, which bring us CSPAN and "Beavis and Butthead," or Howard Stern and All Things Considered, respectively. But television and radio can be more easily controlled than cyberspace can be. The government, through the FCC, controls the franchise for television and radio. There is no "franchise" for the Internet or other forms of online access. It is not easy to set up a pirate television or radio station to broadcast material not acceptable to the FCC. Virtually anyone with a modem can tap into the Internet or a BBS and "broadcast" anything they want.

This situation frightens the hell out of some people, especially since a good chunk of what is being shared out in cyberspace is, shall we say, "adult-oriented." In cyberspace, there are no ticket takers to confirm the age of the viewers, no scrambling devices, and limited blocking mechanisms. This means that children potentially have access to the adult-oriented content of cyberspace, including pornographic and obscene material. It also means that children and adults can come into online contact with people whose intentions might be nefarious and who might use the Net to stalk or harass others.

One response to this reality is currently moving its way through the U.S. Congress under title of the Communications Decency Act of 1995,[12] also known as S.314 (the number of the bill in the Senate). The bill, which has been attached to broader telecommunications deregulation legislation, was introduced by Sen. Jim Exon (D-NE) and is frequently referred to as "the Exon Amendment."

Current law prohibits the use of telephones to make harassing calls and to make indecent audiotext (i.e., "dial-a-porn") available to minors. S.314 would extend these prohibitions to all forms of telecommunication. Most importantly, S.314 would impose criminal penalties on anyone who "makes, transmits, or otherwise makes available any comment, request, suggestion, proposal, image, or other communication" which is "obscene, lewd, lascivious, filthy, or indecent" via the use of a "telecommunications device."[13]

It is the breadth and scope of this wording which has set off a firestorm among free speech advocates and telecommunications providers.[14] The words "makes, transmits, or otherwise makes available" cover everyone along the line of an offending communication, including telephone companies, online services, Internet access providers, independent BBSs and anyone through whose network or site an offending communication passes. The terms "obscene, lewd, lascivious, filthy, or indecent" are legally vague. The definition of obscenity is squishy enough in cyberspace (see the discussion of the Thomas AA-BBS case above). One can imagine great difficulty in attempting to screen for "lewd, lascivious, filthy, or indecent," or in a court attempting to evaluate it after the fact.

Recent amendments to S.314, proposed by Sens. Exon and Gorton (R-WA), offer a number of defenses to prosecution under the broad language quoted above. These defenses include: provision of access only (i.e., without involvement in creation or alteration of the material); lack of editorial control; good faith efforts to provide uses with means to restrict offending communications and to respond to user complaints about offending material; and not being engaged in a commercial activity which has as its "predominant purpose" the provision of offending material.

These defenses go a long way toward mitigating the harsh effects of the bill as originally drafted. Left exposed, perhaps, are the small BBS operators who cannot afford sophisticated blocking technology or to whom, because of their size, editorial control will be imputed. Further, these defenses are just that–defenses. They do not necessarily stop the prosecution from bringing its case, backed by the resources of the government, even if they do provide a successful defense at trial. By then, of course, the defendant could be up to his or her neck in legal fees. And the language of these defense provisions is open to interpretation. What is "editorial control"? "Good faith effort"? "Predominant purpose"? If the bill passes, we can expect to see these matters litigated.

The issue here, though, is perhaps less about the legal effect of the specific language of S.314 than about the concept of free speech in a wired society. The debate right now is being dominated by extremists on either end of the spectrum: those who wrap everything up in a "for the good of our children" argument and those who oppose any governmental control or restriction on speech. In the view of this writer, the problem with S.314 is that it does seem to recognize the interactive, consensual, and decentralized nature of cyberspace. Of course, many people oppose the current restrictions on television and radio content, arguing that those offended can simply change the channel. Further, many commentators question the constitutionality of the "dial-a-porn" restrictions placed into law a few years ago at the initiative of Sen. Jesse Helms. Even if one accepts these restrictions on television, radio, and telephone communication, though, it does not follow that such restrictions should also be imposed in cyberspace or that they will be workable there.

Attempts to control cyberspace, because of its ubiquitous nature, will almost by definition have to be onerous. There seemingly are no delicate ways for the government to intervene in cyberspace. We saw that with the failed Clipper Chip initiative, in which the government sought to have the key to all encrypted communications. We saw that in the Thomas AA-BBS case, in which the long arm of federal law hauled the California couple to Tennessee for prosecution, simply because that is where the user who downloaded the material was located. We see it again with S.314, which, even with the insertion of the new defenses, seeks to impose restrictions on the content of all telecommunications, however consensual, at every step along the way.

One can conclude from these efforts that it will be difficult for the government to protect us from ourselves in cyberspace without impinging on individual responsibilities and civil liberties. The question we should ask ourselves, perhaps, is whether we want or need that protection. And, in the wake of the Oklahoma City bombing, how we should balance the needs of law enforcement with our individual rights of privacy and free speech.

NOTES

The Electronic Frontier Foundation (EFF) is an excellent source for materials relating to S.314, as well as to numerous issues relating to civil liberties and intellectual property protection in cyberspace. Most of the material gathered in researching this article was found in the "Legislation" section of EFF's WWW site. You can reach EFF's homepage at http://www/eff.org.

1. Portions of this article appeared originally in the February 1995 and June 1995 issues of the journal *Against the Grain*, in the author's "Legally Speaking" column.

2. N.Y. Exec. Law sec. 632-a (McKinney 1982 & supp. 1987).

3. 112 S. Ct. 501 (1991). *See* Debra A. Shields, *The Constitutionality of Current Crime Victimization Statutes: A Survey*, 75 Fordham Intellectual Property, Media & Entertainment Law Journal 935-40 (analyzing *Simon & Schuster*); Calvin Reid, *U.S. Supreme Court Strikes Down N.Y. State's 'Son of Sam' Law*, Publishers Wkly., Jan. 1, 1991, at 16-17 (discussing *Simon & Schuster)*.

4. See Shields, supra note 2, at 941 (discussing the post-*Simon & Schuster* amendment of the law and concluding that the amended law is constitutional).

5. *Id.* at 956.

6. *See* Maureen O'Brien, *Simpson Case Confronts Publishers with New Laws*, Publishers Wkly., Apr. 24, 1995, at 10.

7. *Id.*

8. *Id.*

9. *See* Matthew Goldstein, *Prodigy Case May Solve Troubling Liability Puzzle*, The National Law Journal, Dec. 19, 1994, at B1. The case was filed in a New York state court in November 1994. *See also* Sandra Donnelly, *Cyber Smears*, Internet World, May 1995, at 86 (discussing the *Prodigy* case).

10. *Cubby v. CompuServe, Inc.,* 776 F. Supp. 135 (1991).

11. *See Miller v. California*, 413 U.S. 15, 24 (1973). In *Miller*, the Supreme Court determined that a work is obscene if " . . . the average person, applying contemporary community standards . . . finds that the work, taken as a whole, appeals to prurient interest . . . (and) the work taken as a whole lacks serious literary, artistic, political, or scientific value."

12. *See* S. 314, 104th Congress, 1st Session. S. 314 would amend 47 U.S.C. 223.

13. *See* Center For Democracy and Technology, *CDT Policy Post 2/9/95*, accessed in the "Legislation" section of Electronic Frontier Foundation's WWW site (http://www/eff.org).

14. *See* Calvin Reid, *Publishers Protest Scope and Language of Anti-Cybersmut Bill*, Publishers Wkly., April 10, 1995, at 9.

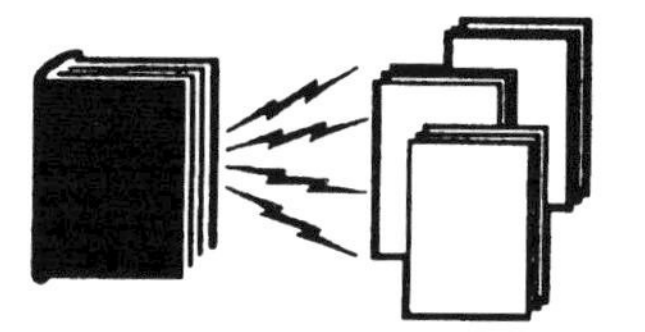

Haworth DOCUMENT DELIVERY SERVICE

This valuable service provides a single-article order form for any article from a Haworth journal.

- *Time Saving:* No running around from library to library to find a specific article.
- *Cost Effective:* All costs are kept down to a minimum.
- *Fast Delivery:* Choose from several options, including same-day FAX.
- *No Copyright Hassles:* You will be supplied by the original publisher.
- *Easy Payment:* Choose from several easy payment methods.

Open Accounts Welcome for . . .

- Library Interlibrary Loan Departments
- Library Network/Consortia Wishing to Provide Single-Article Services
- Indexing/Abstracting Services with Single Article Provision Services
- Document Provision Brokers and Freelance Information Service Providers

MAIL or *FAX* THIS ENTIRE ORDER FORM TO:

Haworth Document Delivery Service
The Haworth Press, Inc.
10 Alice Street
Binghamton, NY 13904-1580

or FAX: 1-800-895-0582
or CALL: 1-800-342-9678
9am-5pm EST

PLEASE SEND ME PHOTOCOPIES OF THE FOLLOWING SINGLE ARTICLES:

1) Journal Title: ______________________________
Vol/Issue/Year: ______________ Starting & Ending Pages: ____________
Article Title: ______________________________
____

2) Journal Title: ______________________________
Vol/Issue/Year: ______________ Starting & Ending Pages: ____________
Article Title: ______________________________
____

3) Journal Title: ______________________________
Vol/Issue/Year: ______________ Starting & Ending Pages: ____________
Article Title: ______________________________
____

4) Journal Title: ______________________________
Vol/Issue/Year: ______________ Starting & Ending Pages: ____________
Article Title: ______________________________
____

(See other side for Costs and Payment Information)

COSTS: Please figure your cost to order quality copies of an article.

1. Set-up charge per article: $8.00
   ($8.00 × number of separate articles) __________
2. Photocopying charge for each article:
   1-10 pages: $1.00 __________
   11-19 pages: $3.00 __________
   20-29 pages: $5.00 __________
   30+ pages: $2.00/10 pages __________
3. Flexicover (optional): $2.00/article __________
4. Postage & Handling: US: $1.00 for the first article/
   $.50 each additional article __________
   Federal Express: $25.00 __________
   Outside US: $2.00 for first article/
   $.50 each additional article __________
5. Same-day FAX service: $.35 per page __________

GRAND TOTAL: ______________

METHOD OF PAYMENT: (please check one)

❑ Check enclosed ❑ Please ship and bill. PO # ____________________

(sorry we can ship and bill to bookstores only! All others must pre-pay)

❑ Charge to my credit card: ❑ Visa; ❑ MasterCard; ❑ Discover;
❑ American Express;

Account Number: ____________________ Expiration date: ____________

Signature: ✗ ________________________________

Name: ____________________ Institution: ____________________

Address: ____

____

City: ____________________ State: ________ Zip: ____________

Phone Number: ________________ FAX Number: ________________

MAIL or *FAX* THIS ENTIRE ORDER FORM TO:

Haworth Document Delivery Service
The Haworth Press, Inc.
10 Alice Street
Binghamton, NY 13904-1580

or FAX: 1-800-895-0582
or CALL: 1-800-342-9678
9am-5pm EST)